Think Yourself Gorgeous

Anita Naik is a freelance writer, author and columnist. She specialises in health and lifestyle issues and has written for a variety of magazines including *Glamour, Closer* and *Now.* She is also the author of over 40 books and was previously the agony aunt on *Just 17* and *Closer* magazines. Anita is currently an editorial board member on the Dove Self-Esteem Fund website. For her blogs and columns on self-esteem go to www.dove.co.uk.

For more information on her books go to www.anitanaik.co.uk.

Anita is also the author of:

Babe Bible
The Lazy Girl's Guide to Beauty
The Lazy Girl's Guide to Good Health
The Lazy Girl's Guide to Good Sex
The Lazy Girl's Guide to a Fabulous Body
The Lazy Girl's Guide to Men
The Lazy Girl's Guide to Success
The Lazy Girl's Guide to Green Living
The Lazy Girl's Guide to High Life on a Budget
The Lazy Girl's Party Guide
The New You
Pocket Babe

Think Yourself Gorgeous

How to feel good – inside and out

Anita
Naik

piatkus

PIATKUS

First published in Great Britain in 2009 by Piatkus

*A CIP catalogue record for this book is available from the
British Library.*

ISBN 978-0-7499-4181-9

Text designed and set by Sam Charrington Design
Illustrations by Robyn Neild
Printed and bound in Great Britain by CPI Mackays, Chatham, ME5 8TD

Papers used by Piatkus are natural, renewable and recyclable products
sourced from well-managed forests and certified in accordance with the
rules of the Forest Stewardship Council.

Mixed Sources
Product group from well-managed
forests and other controlled sources
www.fsc.org   Cert no. SGS-COC-004081
© 1996 Forest Stewardship Council
FSC

Piatkus
An imprint of
Little, Brown Book Group
100 Victoria Embankment
London EC4Y 0DY

An Hachette UK Company
www.hachette.co.uk

www.piatkus.co.uk

Contents

Acknowledgements   ix

Introduction   1

Chapter One
Your Changing Body   5

What is puberty?   8

Self-esteem and puberty   12

Quiz: Is your self-esteem nose-diving   12
because of puberty?

What to expect – the physical changes of puberty   16

Breast issues   18

Body hair issues   22

Period issues   25

Body sweat and body odour   27

Acne and Spots   29

What to expect – the emotional changes of puberty   31

Chapter Two
Body Image SOS   41

The negative influences   42

How do you feel about the real you?   43

The body image slammers – obsessing about   46
your body shape

Quiz: Are you too body-conscious?   47

The body image slammers – diets and dieting   51

The body image slammers – your peer group   54

The body image slammers – feeling you are fat   56

Quiz: How weight-obsessed are you?   57

The body image slammers – eating disorders   62

How to improve your body image   64

The beauty image slammers – your idea of beauty   70

Quiz: How beautiful do you feel?   71

The beauty image slammers – the beauty industry   74

How to improve your beauty image   78

Chapter Three

Gorgeous in the Real World   81

Dealing with best friends, cliques and enemies   82

Quiz: What kind of friend are you?   85

Surviving cliques   86

Handling mean behaviour   89

Friends who are enemies   91

Being an outsider   93

Being the popular girl   96

Improving your friendship skills   98

Dealing with parents   100

Quiz: Who's bringing you down?   100

Mothers and daughters   103

Fathers and daughters   106

Dealing with boys   110

Quiz: Your views on love   111

Sorting out the love myths from reality   113

Dealing with you   116

Quiz: How hard are you on yourself?   116

Chapter Four
Gorgeous for Life 122

Looking after your body   123

The basics of healthy eating   123

Exercise and self-esteem   127

Getting rid of your bad habits   130

Looking after your looks   134

Finding your style   135

How to find your inner beauty   142

Being gorgeous for life   144

Resources   156

Index   162

For Jadie Panayis –
who is gorgeous and good, both inside and out.

Acknowledgements

With thanks to my gorgeous Bella who shouted, 'Mummy turn the computer off' as I wrote this book. I hope that one day this book will help bolster your self-confidence should it ever flag. Also, huge thanks go to Lily and Charlotte Watson, Chloe and Melissa Roske, Jane Naik, Jenni, Cassie and Tara Panayis, all of whom gave me excellent insights into the world of girls and self-esteem. Grateful thanks as well to the girls and women who send me their thoughts on everything from self-esteem to body image and feeling great at the Dove Self-Esteem Fund site www.dove.co.uk. Your views are invaluable.

Introduction

Thinking yourself gorgeous is about how you feel about yourself – in other words: it's about your self-esteem. So what is self-esteem, apart from being an annoying buzzword that perhaps your parents and teachers keep banging on about? Well, in a nutshell it's a term that describes how you feel about yourself, both on the inside and out. It includes how you feel about your body: do you love your bits or loathe your looks? Your personality: are you kind and sensitive or downright mean and nasty? Your intelligence levels: are you a natural genius or an exam loser? Your talents: do you have heaps of them or none whatsoever? The more positive your estimation of yourself, the higher your esteem will be, but on the other hand, the more negative your estimation of yourself, the lower your confidence in yourself will be.

Of course, having good self-esteem and liking yourself 'warts and all' is not really as black and white as the above – or rather it shouldn't be, because none of us is 100 per cent perfect or 100 per cent rubbish at anything (even if the latter sometimes feels that way). The problem is that when you're hitting your teen years, life often feels negative in every way. So, if you're someone who is wracked with self-doubt about everything from your looks to your abilities, and you feel that you're not good enough, pretty enough or smart enough, then rest assured, you're normal.

The problem is that low self-esteem is a multi-layered difficulty and one that not only makes us feel terrible about ourselves but also affects our choices and behaviours in the outside world. It can hold you back from being happy; it can stop you from doing what you want in life; it can make you be horrible to the people you love; and it can make you vulnerable around the people who you should tell to get lost. If you have low self-esteem it's likely you also:

- Put yourself down all the time.
- Find you are scared to try new things.
- Believe you don't have any talents.
- Hold back for fear of messing up.
- Find you are too afraid to assert yourself.
- Often blame others for your problems.

It may seem unimportant to worry about how you feel, but in reality it's essential, because the way you judge yourself now, and the behaviours you adopt to cope with this, set the stage for your adult life. That's because if you feel unworthy and unimportant as a teen, it's likely you'll carry these feelings and behaviours into your grown-up life. By comparison, if you improve your self-esteem, it will help you to make good choices, limit risky behaviour, and generally look after yourself in every way possible, now and in the future. What's more, it will protect you from feeling inadequate and unworthy, and also help you to stand up to peer pressure so that you can do what you believe is right.

Self-esteem is, of course, a massive umbrella term that includes confidence, body image and also self-belief, and, as a result, it's affected by a variety of factors such as who you hang out with, what boys you like, the celebrities you admire and even who your parents are.

Television programmes, adverts, DVDs, films, music and magazines also all add to the mix, sending out images and ideas that are often virtually impossible to live up to (more on that later). On a logical level, it doesn't take a genius to work out that it's stupid to let our feelings about ourselves be affected by these things, but the truth is it's impossible not to let the outside world affect our internal world.

This is where *Think Yourself Gorgeous* comes in. This is literally your guide to how to feel fantastic about who you are, right now. It's about finding the great bits in you while fighting your negative demons. It's also about facing the practicalities of life as a teenage girl, such as how to deal with puberty, stand up to the cliques, battle mean girls and deal with the people that dominate your world and influence your thinking.

As daunting as the above seems, you can get to grips with low self-esteem and be happier and less anxious – and it's easier than you think. Get there and you'll like yourself a lot more, be a better friend, feel gorgeous – and, best of all, feel strong and more content with who you are. You'll be able to stand up to people who make you feel bad and know that whatever others say to you, when it comes down to it you always know yourself best.

So, remind yourself as you work your way through this book that you're tackling the hard stuff, the painful stuff and the annoying stuff because you deserve to feel gorgeous and wonderful and fabulous.

You deserve to be able to look in the mirror without going, 'Yuck!' and most of all you deserve to like who you are inside and out. Learn to like yourself in this way and I guarantee it will make you more gorgeous than you could ever imagine.

Your Changing Body

Some girls love their bodies – and because they feel good about how they look, they ooze confidence. This comes across in everything they do. They are the ones who charge into communal changing rooms to try on clothes, confidently walk about in their underwear post-PE and wear whatever they want to without even considering whether it's an adequate cover-up or not. They don't suck in their stomachs at the swimming pool, they happily wear vest tops without worrying about boob spillage, and they don't sigh loudly when they see what's in fashion next season. And yes, although some of them have been lucky enough to grab all the long-and-lean genes, some of them haven't.

> "What do I like about myself? My friends say my eyes are nice, but I'm definitely too fat and too short. I'm also embarrassed about my breasts and I have chunky legs, so they always look bad. I'd like to be lighter and skinnier and have straight hair."
>
> **Ashley, 13**

The fact is that some girls just love their bodies, no matter what other people think, and, as a result, their lives are a lot less complicated than our own. Of course, the majority of us don't feel that way. Surveys show that by the age of 13 years over half of all teenage girls are dissatisfied with their bodies and how they look, a figure that reaches to over three-quarters of girls by the time they are 17 years old.

Look around you; do you really think that that many girls have a reason to feel this way? It's unlikely isn't it? In fact, do a quick straw poll of your friends and ask yourself the following:

1 How many of your friends moan about their bodies, but you can't see what their problem is?

2 How many friends complain about a body part that you think looks normal?

3 How many body bits do you feel dissatisfied with, although your friends can't see that there is a problem?

If you're someone who feels insecure and dissatisfied about how you look, it's likely that you can write an essay on all the things wrong with you. Perhaps you're annoyed that your tummy ripples rather than staying flat, or you are pretty revolted by everything from the shape of your breasts to the size of your bottom. If so, it's likely you're the person who struggles to get changed inside a towel after PE, and probably opts for a black all-in-one swimsuit instead of a bikini, claiming you like staying neck-deep in the water all day instead of having fun in the sun.

OK, I'll admit it: I've been describing the teenage me in the section above, but I'll bet it's rung a few familiar bells with some of you out there. When I look back now I think, *what a waste of effort*: spending all day in the water until I had prune-like skin just because I was too afraid to walk about in a swimsuit in front of other people. The heartbreaking part of all this is that I wasn't alone, because most of my friends were right there in the water with me, covering up and criticising their bodies in minute detail. Looking back I often wondered what they were on about, because to me they looked pretty good, but they were probably thinking the same about me.

It all changes so fast

The point here is that if you currently hate your body, you're not alone. This is because when it comes to feeling gorgeous, most girls, especially during adolescence, have incredibly conflicting feelings about their bodies. It's a horrible way to feel, especially if you think back just a few years and remember that you probably didn't give that much thought to how you looked. So, what's happened since then? Well, it's likely that puberty has happened and it's changed your body and your thinking overnight.

Puberty has a lot to answer for in the self-consciousness stakes. In many ways it's like a big joke. As your body starts lengthening and widening, and sticking out, your emotions go haywire and you become extra-sensitive and extra-aware. Unfortunately, most of this awareness goes into comparing how badly we fare against other girls and women – and that's not just your friends and the girls at school, but the thousands of images that we see every day, especially the ones of skinny and perfect-looking models, and celebrities.

Who is your role model?

If you think you're not affected by what you see, then think again. One major study by Dove, shows that by the time a girl hits 12 years old, she will have been exposed to more than 77,000 adverts. The study, which surveyed girls in the UK and the US aged between 10 and 14, found that over three-quarters of girls reported feeling fat, unattractive and depressed when faced with pictures of beautiful models and celebrities. More than half of these girls then described themselves as 'disgusting' and 'ugly'.

It's not surprising when you think about it, because what we see not only influences how we feel but also how we behave. So, before you define yourself as too fat/too short/too tall, and so on, you need to ask yourself: how many times have you watched an advert aimed at your age group and been faced with a model who looked like a normal teenage girl – the type of girl who's also hitting the awkward bit of puberty, and the kind of girl you're friends with? The answer is probably never, which, when you think about it, is pretty strange in itself.

Worst still, alongside this overemphasis on how we look, comes a fixation with weight and the belief that being thin is better. Many girls believe that being thin is prettier and that thin girls will definitely be more successful. Small wonder, then, that so many girls feel inferior and inadequate. So, if you want to feel good about yourself, it's vital to understand what's happening to your body and mind, and to let go of your unrealistic expectations.

The starting point is to get to grips with the process of puberty – not just in terms of the biological changes, but also in terms of how the changes are going to make you feel about yourself, and how they will affect your self-esteem and your confidence levels.

What is puberty?

Have you found that as your body changes so too have your feelings about your body, your abilities, your intelligence and your social skills? Do the changes of puberty make your body feel stronger or weaker? Do you feel wiser or less of a person? The chances are that whereas you're wise enough to know what's happening to your body, the changes have left you feeling more than a little at odds with yourself. Perhaps, you're wondering who you are and worrying why you feel so awkward and unsure about your looks and personality.

Maybe your self-confidence has dropped off the scale and you're no longer sure what's so great about being you. You might even wonder what the point of everything is anyway. If so, welcome to puberty! This may be the physical process that changes your body from a child's one into an adult one, but it's also the emotional process that will take you on a rollercoaster ride of highs and lows.

> "My mum told me about the puberty biology bits. Like why we get periods and breasts, and said it was a good healthy sign, but she never said my period would be so horrible and that I'd feel fat and ugly and that my body would look this bad."
>
> **Jess, 14**

When does it start?

For girls, puberty usually begins between the ages of 9 and 13, although sometimes it can be earlier and sometimes later, which can be a problem in itself if it's happening to you. Early puberty is difficult to go through, because it can make you feel awkward and embarrassed. It can even make you feel an outsider among your friends, as your body starts to develop way ahead of everyone else's. Although you will all obviously equal out in the end, hitting puberty early can feel like a lonely and miserable place to be in. This is partly because it can attract unwanted male attention way before you're ready to deal with it and also because it can literally make you feel like you're dealing with things alone.

Late puberty is also very difficult to handle, because it can make you feel unattractive and immature, and that all your friends have left you behind! In reality, though, no one's laughing or looking at you, whether you start early or late, because the truth is that everyone's too busy worrying about what's happening to his or her own body. However, it can help to talk to someone you trust about what's happening to you and ask them to help you with small things that can help to make the transition less uncomfortable.

Early puberty helpers

✦ Wearing a properly fitted bra.

✦ Buying new clothes that fit properly.

✦ Talking to your parents so that they understand what's happening to you.

✦ Talking with friends about how you feel awkward or embarrassed.

Late puberty helpers

✦ Seeing your doctor to reassure you that you are perfectly fine.

✦ Talking to your mum about your fears (she can help with the stuff you feel embarrassed about).

✦ Asking if you can buy more grown-up clothes to fit in with your friends.

✦ Telling friends how you feel.

Coping with the difficulties

Another problem with puberty is boys! This is because boys start puberty later than girls (between the ages of 10 and 15), which is why you might suddenly find that you are taller and bigger than most of the boys in your class – and at the mercy of their juvenile behaviour. The reality is that many boys just don't know how to handle puberty, because they get even less information about it than girls do.

> "I think my mum was unaware of what I was going through because she didn't get me a bra or new clothes. I talked to my aunt about how bad I felt; how boys made fun of my chest and how I felt self-conscious, especially in PE. She talked to my mum and we went shopping together. I didn't feel so exposed once everything fitted better."
>
> **Leanne, 17 (started puberty at 10 years old)**

So, how is a girl to handle all of this? Well, a good place to start is to understand – and to keep telling yourself – that how you look at the beginning or middle of puberty isn't how you're going to end up looking at the end of it. It's not until you're around 16 or 17 years old that puberty really stops and your true look and size is revealed. This is why you shouldn't panic if you're a head taller than every boy and girl at 13 years old, or if you're as flat as a pancake at 15 years old.

Trying to see into the future

To get a rough idea of how you're going to end up looking, take a look at the women in your family. Pictures of your mum, aunts and older sisters when they were teenagers, can give you a hint (notice I say 'hint' rather than an 'accurate profile') of how you might look, because you share some of the same genes. Genes are made up of DNA, which is passed to you by your parents in the womb. The genes carry information about how your body is going to grow and develop.

This doesn't mean that you're going to be a perfect copy of your mum, aunts and sisters, but more that if small breasts/ large breasts/long legs/an athletic build run in the family then there is a good chance you'll have these too. One quick aside: the one area that you shouldn't focus on too much is weight, because this isn't determined by genetic factors but external factors such as lifestyle and age (see Chapter Two for more on this). Also, if you're a late or early starter, check when your mother started puberty, because most girls start around the same age that their mother's did – again this is a genetic factor.

Self-esteem and puberty

Several studies found that when hitting puberty, girls are likely to experience a crisis in confidence that sees their self-esteem plummet. Before finding out why this happens, find out where you are right now on the puberty and self-esteem scale.

Quiz: Is your self-esteem nose-diving because of puberty?

For the following questions tick the answer that seems closest for you, then add up your scores at the end:

1 You win a snowboarding lesson, are you likely to give it a try?
  a. No way! You're not falling over in front of strangers! (0)
  b. No, you're definitely not the sporty type. (5)
  c. Yes, you'll give anything a try. (10)

2 Your school's having a fashion show and needs volunteers to model, are you signing up for it?
  a. No chance! You're too fat to be a model and everyone will laugh. (0)
  b. No, you know the girls who'll be chosen, and it won't be you. (5)
  c. Fashion's not your thing but you're happy to give it a try as it sounds fun. (10)

3 You're asked to join the swimming team. How do you feel?
  a. Over the moon that you've been asked. (10)
  b. Horrified – you feel too overexposed in a swimming costume. (0)
  c. Scared that you're going to fail and let everyone down. (5)

4 **When you were eight years old were you:**
   a. Braver than you are now? (0)
   b. More popular than you are now? (5)
   c. Sillier than you are now? (10)

5 **How do you feel about eating in front of other people you don't know?**
   a. You hate it, so you never do it. (0)
   b. You tend to censor what you eat, so that people don't judge you for it. (5)
   c. It doesn't bother you at all. (10)

Scores

0–15 Nose-diving esteem
Your self-esteem has taken a serious nose-dive and it's likely the start of puberty has made you feel vulnerable, exposed and on show to others. Perhaps someone is judging you harshly or perhaps you're doing it to yourself, but the resulting effect is that it's making you shrink inwards, and basically holding you back.

20–35 Wavering esteem
Your self-esteem has taken a battering and it's wavering between being too low and being OK. What's holding you back is the fear that people won't like you if you show them the real you and that somehow you're simply not good enough.

40–50 Strong self-esteem
Well done! You have a healthy self-esteem, you're not too scared to try something new, and not too worried about what others think. You know what you like and you're not afraid to stick to your guns, and be who you are.

Puberty can make you miserable

For most girls, misery and dissatisfaction with their body and who they are starts at puberty, because one of the first signs that puberty has arrived is a sudden spurt in growth, both in height and weight, and the start of breast development. This means that whereas you might once have looked like everyone else you know, suddenly you'll have breasts that are noticeable, and curves around your hips and thighs, caused by your body laying down fat. Apart from being alarming, these are difficult changes to come to terms with, especially if you liked they way you looked before, and you don't feel ready to be this new person. All of this is made worse by internal and external factors such as:

How your hormones influence your thinking

During puberty your hormone levels surge and fall daily to accommodate the many bodily changes going on. This is why you may feel like crying one minute and laughing another. It's a bit like having permanent PMS for three years (see Period Issues on page 25 below for more on this). It's completely understandable why you swing rapidly from one emotion to another. The solution is to go with it: be nice to yourself (that is, give yourself a break for feeling this way) and sometimes just have a good cry so that you can feel better. The good news is that you are not going to feel this way forever.

> "I don't know what's wrong with me;
> everything makes me cry. I look at
> myself in the mirror and feel tears
> welling up. Yesterday I couldn't fit into
> my old jeans and ended up crying for
> half an hour. My mum said it's normal to
> feel this way and I know that, but I
> just feel so sad all the time."
> **Jo, 12**

Puberty is such a public process

Another problem is that puberty is a very obvious and public process, and, as a result, you'll feel sensitive to what others say and think about you. Although that's totally understandable, there is also a very annoying number of adults who will comment and say insensitive things like: 'Goodness haven't you got big?', 'Gosh, that's a big spot' and 'Should you be eating that?' – and then they wonder why you're upset. The solution is to tell people that they are hurting your feelings and not let them get away with insensitive comments about your body. The reality is that adults really should know better, and if you don't feel you can speak up, ask your mum to have a quiet word. If she's the culprit, remind her how she used to feel, and tell her how the teasing is getting you down.

The changes of puberty are uncomfortable

Growing taller, having to deal with breasts when you had none before, and feeling that your body is doing things without your permission are just some of the reasons why you might feel at odds with your body. Clumsiness is also a by-product of this, especially if you have a growth spurt almost overnight. The solution is to take practical measures; for example, make sure you get measured for the correct bra size (for more on this see Breast Issues on page 18) and if you're suffering from growing pains (these are totally real, as puberty makes your bones ache) see your GP for advice and help.

Puberty makes you tired

It's funny, but when you were a baby and going through a growth spurt, the adults around you were likely to be sympathetic to your need to sleep, chill out and relax. It's a shame they are not so sympathetic when you're in your teens. The fact is that puberty is exhausting and tiring, which means you really do need more sleep and more downtime. Another reason you need more sleep is because the hormones associated with growth are secreted during sleep at higher levels than when you're awake (which is why young babies sleep so much). So give yourself a break, and if your parents accuse you of being lazy, point out the above.

Puberty makes you doubt yourself

This is simply because up until now you've had about ten years or more to get used to your body, and know inside and out what it can do, and what you're good at. At puberty, even though you are still you, a changing body can make you feel vulnerable and insecure. This might make you start doubting your physical abilities, opting to avoid sport and being less active, because it makes you feel clumsy and exposed. The solution is to remember that everyone is going through the same thing, and if you don't fancy the sports you used to do, try to find something that suits the new you instead. Why? Well, because studies show that girls who take part in sport (that's 'take part', not necessarily 'excel' in it or win a medal) have more body confidence and higher self-esteem than those who sit on the sidelines every week pretending they have their period.

What to expect – the physical changes of puberty

While you may know some of the changes to expect with puberty, you probably don't know all of them and exactly why they happen. This section is designed to reveal all and at the same time help you to feel reassured by what's happening so that you don't feel freaked out, scared or worried.

Puberty and the fat factor

Puberty growth fact: during puberty your head, hands and feet are the first things to grow. Then your arms and legs grow, and finally your torso and shoulders catch up with the rest of your body.

Gaining weight for many girls is the main fear with puberty, but it's an exaggerated one that is often fuelled by peer pressure and what we see on TV and in magazines. The truth is that during the four years that puberty lasts, you will become 25 per cent taller and this height growth is accompanied by an increase in weight. Weight gain is a perfectly normal part of puberty, because without it your body cannot grow taller, develop breasts, or trigger your first period.

To help yourself, remember that:

⭐ **You're likely to be uncomfortable** about the look of your body, but this is normal. Think of ways you can help yourself, such as buying better-fitting clothes and changing the way you dress so that you don't feel so self-conscious.

⭐ **You may not like your reflection** – mainly because you're looking at yourself in a very critical way and usually focusing on the bits you hate. Remember: the parts you loathe look bigger because you're focusing on them. For every negative part try to find a contrasting positive part of your body and spend the same amount of time focusing on that.

⭐ **Your appetite might increase** because your body needs more calories to fuel the changes of puberty. Again, consider how much an eight-year-old eats compared to a 13-year-old. If you want to be healthy, eat a wide range of foods with a little bit of what you like, and you'll be fine.

⭐ **You're going to feel sensitive** when people comment on your body, because we all do, no matter what our age. Again, if someone is teasing you or saying insensitive things, speak up and tell them how it's making you feel. It's not a joke if it hurts your feelings.

During puberty you'll gain about 18kg (40lb), which sounds a huge amount, but the weight gain consists of muscle, bone and organs as well as fat. To get an idea of what this means, take a look at a seven- or eight-year-old and compare the difference in their size and body shape to a 15- or 16-year-old. You'll see how the weight gain is about growth and not about getting fat.

What's also important to realise is that weight gain will usually happen before height gain, because fat plays a vital role in the start of your periods (body fat helps trigger the hormones that start menstruation). This means, for a short period you may notice what's known as 'baby fat' around your middle and hips. This can cause a large amount of anxiety, so remind yourself that as soon as you grow taller the fat will disappear.

What's more, the shape you start out being at the beginning of puberty is not the shape you'll end up being when you're 17 years old. So, hard as it is, don't become weight fixated and worry that you need to start dieting. Restricting your food intake, over-exercising and standing on the scales every day is a recipe for plunging self-esteem (see Chapter Two for more on this) and an appalling body image that can last way beyond puberty.

Breast issues

We live in a breast-obsessed world and, as a result, it's really easy to put too much emphasis on the size and shape of your breasts and imagine that you're not attractive if your breasts are too small or if you're too big. The fact is it doesn't matter if you have big or small breasts, a pert or less pert pair – they are just breasts, and they don't define who you are. Made up of milk glands and ducts, tissue and fat, breasts are there to produce milk if you ever decide to have a baby, but of course they do affect you in the self-confidence stakes as well.

What's normal?

The reasons why your breasts can get you down have much to do with the media images of what's sexy and what isn't that we're presented with. In the 1950s, bigger busts were in; in the 1960s, flat boobs were sexy; in the 1970s, boobs that

were hanging low, free and loose were hot. These days, however, a spectacular pair of breasts usually means a false plastic surgery pair. As a result we tend to think that good breasts have to be firm, relatively big and pert – a physiological no-no when you think about it.

Even if you have smaller than average breasts, it's unlikely that they'll ever be as pert as a plastic pair, and if you have a bigger pair, gravity isn't going to let them stay upright and pert. All of which means that we all need to get real about boobs and stop worrying that ours don't look like the ones celebrities have paid for.

What happens as they grow?

Breast fact: there is no muscle tissue in the breast, which is why breast exercises can't improve the pertness or size of your breasts. You can however, improve the muscle tone under your breasts and this can help lift your breasts slightly. The best way to do this is with regular activity and exercise that helps tone all of your body.

Breast development itself is the first sign of puberty, and the timing of their growth is pre-determined by your personal body clock, which means that the process can't be rushed or slowed down. When your breasts first start growing, the breast tissue is firm, but this changes as you get older, because breasts are essentially made up of fat and not muscle. So, as your weight changes, so too will your breast size.

When your breasts first start budding they will be very tender, and as the skin stretches you may even find that you get stretch marks. This occurs when breast growth is very fast and your skin doesn't have time to stretch slowly, so the tissue under the skin tears. It's not painful, but it can be alarming to see. However, stretch marks, which can appear anywhere on the body (your back, legs, bottom and stomach) as purple or red, thin scars, do eventually fade, so you don't have to worry too much about them.

In terms of getting to grips with breast growth, the following can help you feel more body-confident:

1. Get measured for a bra

Being measured for a bra is free in all department stores and it's less embarrassing than you might think, because you don't have to strip off for it. Get the right bra size and you'll be laughing, because not only will you feel less self-conscious but also your breasts will be totally supported, so you'll feel the weight of them a lot less. Despite this, the majority of women guess at their bra size. As a result, studies show that 85 per cent of women wear the wrong size, which is bad news for them because an incorrectly fitted bra will be uncomfortable and it doesn't help them to look their best either. The right bra size will not only give you shape but will also make having breasts more comfortable for sports and when you're wearing more fitted clothes.

Bear in mind, though, that during puberty you have to get measured regularly, so don't go crazy and buy lots of bras at once, as your bra size is likely to change every six months, or even more frequently than this, as your height and weight increases.

2. Understand that breasts grow slowly for around four years

Having said the above, it doesn't mean you're going to grow steadily from an A cup to a DD cup in six months, so don't panic; all it means is your breast size (which includes the measurement around your back as well as the size of your breasts) will slightly increase every six months. So, it's wise to get measured twice a year to make sure your bra fits correctly.

You won't know your final bra size until you're around 17, so don't panic in the meantime if your breasts look huge or too small – the size will even out and the end result will be right for you. As for the growth process there is nothing you can do to make your breasts grow bigger or faster, so don't be fooled by creams or lotions saying they can increase your size or firmness. They are just taking advantage of your fears and are a waste of money.

3. All breasts start out lopsided

It's completely normal to have one breast a different size from the other in the same way that you can have one foot slightly bigger than the other. While your breasts are growing, this is a common worry for girls, because one breast can start growing before the other. In most cases, only you will notice but if you are very worried, see your doctor for reassurance and make sure you get fitted for the right bra size.

4. Don't play the comparison game

The trouble with constantly comparing yourself to others is that it always leaves you feeling either inadequate or smug, neither of which does much for your self-esteem. To feel good about what you've got you have to first accept what you've been given. This doesn't mean being instantly happy about your new look but more that you shouldn't blame your breasts for everything you haven't got (such as a boyfriend, a modelling contract, an ability to wear skimpy tops, and so on).

5. Be aware of what real breasts look like

In a recent study, teenage girls were asked to look at pictures of women's breasts and say which ones they felt looked the most real. Unfortunately, 90 per cent chose a fake pair, so here's the low-down on what real breasts look like and feel like, so you won't feel you've been given a raw deal when yours start to appear:

- Real breasts jiggle when you walk and run.
- Real breasts fall sideways when you lie down.
- Real breasts don't stay upright and pert, especially if they are bigger than a B cup.
- Real breasts feel soft and squishy.

Nipple issues

It's also worth talking about nipples here, because they are often a missed-out part of puberty information. Nipples not only come in a variety of shades – from light pink, to dark pink to brown (usually dependent on your skin colour) – but also a variety of sizes. To begin with they can look quite big, as your breasts will begin to bud beneath them, but as your breasts grow, your nipples will appear smaller and look in proportion to your breast size.

What some girls may find worrying is having what's known as inverted nipples (nipples that turn inwards). This is a completely normal variation of breast development that sometimes will change once puberty is completed, or even later if you decide to get pregnant and breastfeed. It's not a problem and won't need surgery, but if you are worried, see your doctor or your school/surgery nurse for reassurance.

You may also notice what look like tiny bumps and spots on your nipples. Again, these are totally normal and known as Montgomery glands. They are there to secrete an oily substance to protect your breasts when you breastfeed after having a baby.

If you feel embarrassed about erect nipples, it pays to be aware of what causes them. In most cases cold air and rough fabric, and even someone accidentally brushing against you, can cause your nipples to get hard. A slightly padded bra can stop other people noticing this, but don't worry too much about it, as the more you think about it the worse it gets.

Body hair issues

Body hair, whether you like it or loathe it, is going to be with you for life from puberty onwards and, depending on where you live in the world, you're either going to view it as a nasty that has to be shaved, waxed or lasered away, or as a natural part of who you are. What people rarely tell you is that having body hair is something everyone has (it's just more noticeable on some people because of their ethnic background) and that it's really not a big deal, despite all the adverts suggesting you have to remove it.

The growth of your pubic hair is one of the first signs of puberty and you'll notice it happening because it's itchy (this is because of the hair breaking through the skin), but it won't fully grow overnight. To begin with, all you will have is probably just a few fine hairs and later the hair will become thicker and curlier.

Body hair fact: pubic hair won't grow down your leg because it only grows for up to six months at a time before it falls out and starts growing all over again. However, this hair loss isn't noticeable, as it doesn't happen all at once.

Body hair, which also includes hair under the arms, leg hair and even facial hair, is for most girls a sensitive issue, especially as having too much body hair is often portrayed as being masculine and unattractive. What's important to realise is that the amount and the colour of your body hair is determined by your cultural make up, with some people naturally predisposed to having thicker and darker body hair than others. The good news with body hair is that if you feel it's a problem, it is one that is easily fixed (see below) but if you feel your body hair is excessive, it's worth seeing your doctor for reassurance.

To feel more confident about your body hair realise that:

- In some countries, especially in the Mediterranean and Europe, body hair is considered attractive.
- Boys have just as much body hair as you do.
- You shouldn't follow the crowd – you don't have to shave your underarm hair or the hair on your legs if you don't want to.
- You should step away from the mirror especially with regard to your facial hair. Peering really closely at your skin is akin to putting it under a microscope and is not the same as seeing it as it really is.
- Get real about the images you're seeing. Celebrities rarely look hairy because their body hair is plucked, lasered and shaved away. If any makes it through that process, it's digitally removed by a computer so that the skin looks 100 per cent flawless in magazines and posters (and strangely plastic and unreal!).

What to do about your body hair

Different body hair needs different treatment – and some needs to be left as it is.

Pubic hair

Never shave it off. It will only grow back and be hideously itchy. If you're embarrassed about pubic hair peeking out when you go swimming, you can trim it with scissors, consider a bikini wax (but ask your mum first) or use a hair removal cream. If you go for the latter, read the instructions carefully and always test it on a small area first to see if your skin can take it. If your skin goes very red and itchy, avoid using the cream, as it's likely your skin is too sensitive.

A bikini wax is where the hairs around your knicker line are waxed away so that stray hairs don't poke out around the sides. Waxing lasts about six weeks and then you have to do it again. You may have heard of the Brazilian and the Hollywood wax where women literally have their pubic hair reduced to a fine line or waxed away all together. If that sounds painful, it's because it is – but this is a fashion thing and not something you should think about going for.

Underarm and leg hair

Not everyone chooses to get rid of leg or underarm hair. Once again, it's a personal decision. If you do decide to get rid of it, remember that once you start you have to do it regularly. Shaving is the most common type of hair removal, particularly for armpits and legs. It's relatively easy to do and doesn't cost too much money. However, you do need to be *very* careful when using a razor, because it's very easy to cut the skin. The best way to shave is to use soap or a shaving gel first to soften the hair, and then shave in a downward or upwards motion (never across – it sounds obvious, but you'd be amazed at how many people do this without thinking).

Waxing has more of a long-lasting effect than shaving. It works by pulling hair out by the roots using strips of hot wax. Although this can be painful (because of the ripping action, rather than the heat of the wax) it can last up to three to four weeks. You can buy home wax kits or have it done in a salon, but it's expensive. Another downside to waxing is that you have to then let the hair grow back to a certain length before waxing again.

Hair removal creams (also known as depilatory creams) work by burning off unwanted hair but need to be used very carefully (for more on this see Pubic hair above).

Facial hair

NEVER EVER SHAVE FACIAL HAIR OR USE HAIR REMOVAL CREAM OVER ALL OF YOUR FACE. Sorry for the capitals, but it's a point worth making loud and clear, because there are countless stories of girls doing this with painful consequences. Shaving facial hair will give you stubble, and hair removal cream is only meant for a small area of your face (the area above the top lip), use it all over and you risk irritation and permanent damage to your skin. Hard as it is to believe, facial hair is normal and all of us have a fine covering of it on our faces. If you don't believe this, it's likely you have darker hair that is more noticeable on your skin.

If you want to get rid of the hair on your top lip and don't like the sound of hair removal cream, you can always bleach it. Chemical bleaches lighten the hair so that you can't see it. However, bleach tends to make your hair go blond, so if you are dark skinned this can make it show up even more.

Period issues

Period fact: you bleed a lot less than you think during a period, usually only 1 or 2 tablespoons of blood. It just seems like a lot because you're not used to it. If you are worried you are bleeding too much, you can always see your doctor for reassurance.

Periods are funny things: you can't wait to start and probably don't want to be the last person in your class to get yours, but once they come you wish they'd just go away. Your period (also known as menstruation) will usually start between the ages of 11 and 14, and when it starts it will last for between five and seven days and return every 28 to 30 days until you hit the menopause in your fifties. What this means is that in a lifetime the average girl will have about 500 periods, so it pays to get your head around them.

Firstly, how you view your periods is usually dependent on how the women in your family and your friends talk about them. If they complain, view them negatively and make you feel that periods are a female burden, that's how yours will feel. In reality, however, although periods can be painful and uncomfortable, they are amazing things. They not only show that your body is healthy and fertile but when you're having a period they shouldn't affect you physically in any way whatsoever (aside from a few period pains which feel like cramps), which means you can pretty much do everything and anything you want.

Periods, however, are likely to affect your self-esteem for a number of reasons. Firstly, at the beginning a period can make you feel horribly self-conscious and even dirty, which is why it's important to know that (1) no-one can tell that you're on; and (2) menstruation isn't dirty in any way. Secondly, as periods are hormonally led, they will affect your mood usually 10–12 days before your period starts (see below).

Mood changes

Experiencing a range of emotional and physical symptoms, like bloating, headaches, tearfulness and mood swings is known as pre-menstrual syndrome (PMS). There are a total of 150 known symptoms of PMS, but you won't get them all – and in fact you may never get any.

What you might notice is a complete dip in your confidence and you might find that your usual worries and fears become larger and more exaggerated, and even seem to upset you more. Again, this is completely normal, and as soon as your period starts you'll notice your misery will go away. It's also completely normal to feel bloated and bigger than usual just before your period starts. This is because you can gain between 900g (2lb) and 1.3kg (3lb) in water before your period. This happens to prepare your body naturally so that it doesn't become dehydrated while you have your period. The good news is that you will lose all the extra pounds as soon as your period starts again.

The real problem with PMS is that most of us forget it's happening from month to month until we're deep in the middle of it again. So, it can help to keep a diary of your emotions, then when you feel your self-esteem flagging you can check to see if it's PMS, or something else all together.

Body sweat and body odour

It's also easy to become fixated on how you smell during puberty, and this in itself can kick your self-esteem when it's down. The fact is, there is a natural body odour to all of us, but not one that should have you wrinkling your nose in disgust. If it does, you can rid yourself of nasty whiffs with a daily shower, clean clothes (dirty clothes being the number-one reason why people smell) and an antiperspirant. Having said that, being worried that you pong or are giving off a strong odour is a common fear, and one that's been planted in our brains by adverts telling us we need a multitude of beauty products to stop people running away from us.

So here's the science bit. Everyone has two types of sweat glands: eccrine and apocrine. The eccrine glands are found all over the body and produce a mixture of water and salt, the aim of which is to cool the body down. This process is essential so that we don't overheat and pass out. It has no odour, but it does start to smell when bacteria on the skin's surface begin to mix with it.

Body sweat fact: sweat is odourless – it's actually bacteria adding to it that creates the unpleasant smell.

What to do about body odour

1 The solution to BO is good hygiene. Clean clothes are vital, as dirty clothes carry bacteria, which when mixed with sweat turns into BO, and this clings to the fabric. Try to wear clothes that are made from breathable fabrics such as cotton rather than synthetic fabrics, which cause more sweat.

2 Use an antiperspirant. Opting for an antiperspirant as opposed to a deodorant (which is just a perfume spray) can also help, as it will reduce the level of perspiration. You don't have to overspray – just one shot before you go out will do.

3 Shaving regularly in areas that are prone to perspiration, such as the underarms, can reduce the intensity of body odour. The main reason why shaving helps is that hairy regions are ideal places for bacteria to flourish.

4 Avoid going OTT on beauty products. Using a variety of products that contain strong and different fragrances – such as soap, body cream, antiperspirants and perfume – can create an even more pungent combination of offputting smells.

5 Avoid all vaginal deodorants and douches (a rinsing process) – you don't need them and they can cause vaginal yeast infections. Plus, the vagina has a normal musky smell and it's not meant to smell of perfume. If you feel there is an unpleasant smell and/or discharge see your doctor (you can ask to see a female one). It could be a sign that you have a yeast infection such as thrush. It's not a sexual disease and anyone can get it so don't be embarrassed because it can be easily cured.

6 De-stink your feet. Your feet reek, because they sweat a lot. Each foot has more than 250,000 sweat glands, and things like stress or simply having dirty feet can make them sweat and smell even more, so it's a good idea to wash your feet regularly. What you wear on your feet can also affect how much they sweat and/or smell. Certain natural fibres allow air to pass through and help your feet air out a bit. Cotton socks and shoes that aren't made of vinyl or plastic are much better. Also, if you don't wear the same pair of shoes for two days in a row, they will have a chance to air out and that will stop your feet from smelling.

The apocrine glands are found only in the armpits, belly-button area, ears, groin and nipples. The sweat these glands produce is released in response to stress, emotion and sexual excitement, all of which happen randomly at puberty, which is why it's so noticeable. The problem with the apocrine glands is that the sweat released here is stronger than the sweat from the eccrine glands, so when bacteria mixes with it, it releases a very strong and distinct smell of BO, and that's why some teenagers smell more at puberty.

Acne and spots

The word 'acne' is just another name for spots and is another physical by-product of puberty. The good news is:

- What you eat doesn't cause spots.
- What you do doesn't cause spots.
- How much you wash doesn't cause spots.

Spots are a chronic condition caused by your body's hormones. What happens at puberty is the hormones that control oil production in the skin go into overdrive and when this happens excess oil clogs up your skin pores and a spot occurs. After puberty the hormones that cause acne are balanced, so the above doesn't happen, which is why you eventually grow out of spots (you don't get them before puberty because your body doesn't have high levels of sex hormones). If you're lucky enough to have just a few spots you shouldn't worry, as very few people are blessed with flawless skin, despite what you see on adverts. Most spots can be treated with over-the-counter medication and covered up with make-up or a moisturising cream that has a slight tint to it.

If you have very severe acne, it is likely to really affect how you feel about yourself and your confidence levels, which is why you shouldn't suffer in silence. Although you will grow out of it, you don't have to wait. Your doctor can prescribe antibiotics and other medication that can get rid of your spots (although these can take up to six months to kick in, so don't give up).

Spots – what not to do

What not to do with spots is obvious, but hard: don't pick them. This only spreads the bacteria and spots, leaving you with scars and turning a small spot into an even bigger one. The best way to avoid picking is not to peer at your face for endless hours in the mirror, as all this does is magnify your spots, stamp on your confidence levels and make yourself feel deeply unattractive.

Apart from hurtful comments from strangers and so-called 'best friends', the people who may have the most to say about your spots are your parents. If they constantly mention them or try to tell you they are the result of unhealthy eating habits (a parental favourite) it can help to tell them that their comments make you feel self-conscious and bad about yourself. It can also help to give them a leaflet (or this section) about acne so that they can see that your spots are a part of puberty designed to drive you mad!

What to expect – the emotional changes of puberty

Alongside the physical changes of puberty, are a whole range of emotional changes that you may not know about, partly because adults forget about them when they are talking about puberty and partly because as a society we rarely talk about emotional health. This section, therefore, is a taster of some of the emotional feelings and problems you might experience in puberty.

> "I just feel disconnected from my family, my friends and who I used to be. I feel like a freak that no one understands, not even myself."
> **Megan, 12**

Mood swings

Puberty is a stressful time emotionally as well as physically. This is because, thanks to your raging hormones, life becomes a rollercoaster ride of ups and downs where one minute you feel great and the next you feel sad. It's all a result of the way hormones at puberty affect your feelings in an exaggerated way, which in turn affects the way you behave and respond to others. This is why a comment, which you would once have brushed aside, can sting and leave you feeling hurt and eager to lash out.

On top of this, the need to fit in can leave you feeling sensitive to remarks, especially those made about your body, and can make you hear things in the wrong way or take other people's criticisms to heart. All of which plays a significant role in stamping on your levels of self-esteem. Alongside this is the pressure to behave in a grown-up way, pass your exams, and cope with a society that seems to value looks, thinness and clothes above being yourself. It can all leave you feeling as if you're going crazy.

Apologies for making it all sound so dire, but the above are just some of the reasons why you may find yourself going through stressful emotional times. However, what's important to know is that, just like your physiological changes, your emotions will settle down. So, although you may be on a see-saw of emotions right now, there will come a point where everything balances up and you will start to feel more in control again.

However, it is worth knowing that more girls than boys suffer from erratic mood swings during puberty, because female hormones tend to fluctuate more rapidly than the male hormones, and these can cause you to become over-sensitive, tearful and, at turns, aggressive. It's a tormenting emotional mix and it's often upsetting, as emotions such as anger, sadness and depression can be overwhelming and hard to handle and so lead to self-destructive behaviour.

One way of getting to grips with your moods is to see if they follow a pattern. The most obvious mood pattern is linked to your menstrual cycle (see the Mood Chart below), but there are also daily hormonal patterns linked to your energy cycle; that is, are you a morning or an evening person? Knowing which one you are can help you to see when your worst moods are more likely to appear and you can do something about it, such as going to bed earlier. Mood swings will also happen when you're hungry and stressed, as these can also cause your hormones to go into overdrive.

To help yourself, keep a daily diary of how you feel over a two-month period and see if you can spot your daily and monthly pattern of emotions.

The Mood Chart

If you want to chart your moods try linking it to this mood chart. It's a basic outline of how our moods go up and down over the menstrual month. It's a rough guide because it's designed around a 28-day cycle and you may find you have a longer or shorter cycle (both completely normal).

Days 1–7 (day 1 being the first day of your actual period)

1	2	3	4	5	6	7

Mood scale: You're likely to feel relaxed, and happy. This is all down to the release of a hormone from the brain's pituitary gland called FSH (follicle stimulating hormone). This hormone stimulates your ovaries and leads to the production of the female sex hormone: oestrogen.

Days 7–14

7	8	9	10	11	12	13	14

Mood scale: You're likely to feel confident and full of energy, as you're heading towards mid-cycle, and ovulation and oestrogen is high.

Days 14–21

14	15	16	17	18	19	20	21

Mood scale: Post ovulation you're likely to feel some changes on the physical front, you might begin to notice some weight gain, especially around your breasts and stomach (as explained on page 27).

Days 21–28

21	22	23	24	25	26	27	28

Mood scale: You may experience PMS symptoms and tiredness, as your body gets ready for your period.

Spot your emotional triggers

Emotional triggers are just like the trigger on a gun: something, or someone, probably unintentionally pushes a sensitive button and this sets something off inside us, which then causes our mood to instantly shift, and we get mad or sad or depressed. Our triggers (and we all have them, no matter what our age) are based on upsetting past experiences and memories that we find painful. These triggers can be pushed every day during puberty, leaving us to go into instant over-reaction.

For example:

Your mum might say: 'Are you wearing that?'
You feel: she is negatively judging me and thinks I look horrible. This then probably evokes times when she has made you feel like this before and so you respond with fury out of proportion to your mum's comment.

Sadly, our emotional triggers tend to be pushed by people we have close relationships with, partly because they know how to do it and also because it's likely their opinion means more to us and so we're on the look out for judgements. To identify your triggers in the conversations you have with friends, siblings, parents, teachers and boys, look for the following thoughts and emotions:

- Feeling unworthy.
- Feeling incredibly hurt.
- Feeling judged and misrepresented.
- Feeling useless.
- Feeling you're a bad person.
- Feeling you're a failure in someone's eyes.
- Feeling you're doing something wrong.

How to cope with the triggers

To deal with your triggers it's important to first recognise that they have been pushed, and then to stop and think where your thought process is going before responding. For example, using the above scenario, when your mother questions you about your clothes, is she:

1 Judging you?
2 Trying to find out why you're dressed the way you are?
3 Or simply making conversation?

By stopping your automatic thought process you can calm down and think about what she means before giving her the right response and leaving feeling angry and hurt. If you're really unsure what someone means, you can simply ask them to clarify what they're saying by asking, 'What do you mean?'

On a deeper level, feeling judged by the people we like and love (and even by people we don't like) and hearing criticisms in everything others say to us is a strong indicator of low self-esteem. When we don't feel good about the person we are, it's all too easy to imagine that everyone else thinks we are rubbish as well. When that happens we see and hear slights everywhere. So one way to deal productively with the emotional triggers that make you feel bad is to work on improving your own thoughts about yourself.

Start by reminding yourself that no one can make you feel bad, unless you (1) allow them to; and (2) feel bad about yourself already. Think of it this way: if you know you're clever and someone says you are stupid, you're not going to get angry or lose any sleep over it because you know it's a load of rubbish. If, on the other hand, someone questions your intelligence and you worry that you aren't the brightest spark in the pack, it's going to upset you and make you behave in a defensive manner. The same goes for any aspect of yourself that you feel doesn't make the grade: your looks, weight, beauty, personality – the list is endless. Which is why, instead of focusing on what others say to you, you need to focus on what you're saying to yourself (more on this in Chapter Two). Once you can see how you're your own worst enemy and change your inner dialogue, you'll be able to change your responses to your emotional triggers.

Mean behaviour

One of the main developmental stages of puberty is the need to separate emotionally from your parents so that you can mature and become a person in your own right. This is not about changing how you feel about your parents, but it is about separating who you are as a person, from who they are. The way this happens is you will begin to see them as real people with flaws and differing ideas to you. Unfortunately, this separating process is not an easy one and is often fraught with friction, as your parents try to assert authority over you and you try to break away.

Part of the problem is that your parents won't be ready for you to challenge them or do challenging things. Plus, it's likely your method of delivery is going to be less than perfect. If you express your feelings, thoughts and beliefs through anger, sulks, mean comments, personal attacks and rages (the usual arsenal of most teenagers), then life at home is going to be an emotional battlefield. The downside of which is your moods are going to veer steeply as your emotions run from fury to guilt to resentment and back again.

The solution is to try to limit your mean behaviour and defensive thinking. Just because you're changing and your parents are finding it hard doesn't mean that you're a bad person or that they dislike you. If you have parents who judge you harshly, then try to remember that often other people's judgements (even your parents') are really about their own issues; for example, the mother that berates you for what you eat, is likely to be overly conscious of her own weight. The key here is to tell people how you're hearing their comments and listen to how they are hearing yours. For example:

Your mother says: 'Are you eating again?'
You feel: she thinks I am fat and can't control myself.
Your reaction: to get angry with her and eat even more.
Your mother's reaction: bafflement, as she can't understand why you're so angry.

Instead, when your mother makes a comment that stings or irritates:

Think before you react – what is she trying to say? If you can't work it out, ask her what she means. Is she trying to get you to eat more healthily or just making a comment?

Tell her how her comment makes you feel. Has she realised she's making you feel bad or is she completely unaware of how sensitive you are about food and eating (if so, it's time to talk)? Listen to what she says to you instead of assuming you know what she's thinking.

Self-destructive behaviour

This one is a biggie (which is why it's covered in various places all over this book and in Chapter Four), but it's worth knowing that one of the big emotional changes during puberty is that you'll begin to let your feelings about yourself affect your behaviour and actions towards yourself. This means that the worse you feel about yourself, the worse this behaviour is likely to be. Self-destructive behaviour covers a huge range of actions, but the following are the more common ones:

- Hurting yourself physically – cutting, eating disorders, drinking and drugs.
- Hurting your relationships with peers – fighting, mean behaviour, bullying.
- Hurting your reputation – sexual activity, bad behaviour.
- Hurting your record at school – failing exams, being disruptive, not going to school.
- Hurting people you love – arguing, fighting, making home life unbearable.

Being self-destructive can be a cry for help or a sign that your esteem has dropped off the chart and that you don't think you're worth very much. Whatever the reason behind your behaviour, it is vital to seek help and advice. Counselling, confidential helplines, confiding in adults you trust, can all help alleviate the misery behind self-destructive actions as well as helping you to find solutions to why you are on a downward spiral.

The first step is recognising what you're doing and the second is asking for help. Some of these problems can't be solved overnight, but the second you start talking to someone you will start to feel better.

Depression

It is estimated that 10 per cent of 14- to 16-year-olds suffer from significant emotional problems at puberty, ranging from depression to eating disorders. Whereas feeling blue, low and sad at times are a normal part of puberty, caused in part by your changing body and the onslaught or hormones, being depressed is a very different thing.

There are definite signs that you are depressed. Perhaps the biggest one is your feeling of low self-worth. If you feel useless, a failure, have a distorted sense of what your body looks like and feel completely alone and without hope, then your chances of becoming depressed increase. Whereas no single thing causes depression, bear in mind that if you are constantly surrounded by negativity (yours or other people's) or feel very stressed, this could also lead to depression. Other symptoms of depression include:

- Feeling disconnected from everyone.
- Being without hope.
- Oversleeping or insomnia.
- Change in appetite.
- Signs of self-harm, such as cutting yourself.
- Unexplained crying bouts.
- Cutting yourself off from friends.
- A negative change in behaviour at school.
- Having a history of depression in your family.
- Suicidal thoughts.

The good news is that depression is treatable, so the main thing is to recognise that you are depressed and to seek help as soon as possible. Talking with a trusted adult, a therapist and your GP is something that will really help you to unravel your feelings and start feeling good again.

Anger and self-hate

It's rare for a person to go through life and not have moments of self-doubt about who they are and how they look. The problem at puberty, however, is that this thought pattern is exaggerated by the effects of what you're going through. There may well be times when you just can't stand yourself, hate what you say and do, and loathe the way you look. Trying the following things can help alleviate moments of normal self-hate:

- Calling up your best friend and ranting to her, and letting her make you feel better.
- Keeping a diary to let your feelings out.
- Doing some heart-pumping exercise, such as a bike ride or a swim, to take your mind off things.
- Watching a DVD that makes you laugh or feel good.
- Going to someone you love for comfort.
- Giving yourself a five-minute pep talk to make yourself feel good.
- Remembering you don't have to look, act or be perfect.

> "I fight with my mum a lot. She annoys me – the way she speaks and how she's always trying to help me. My dad's always saying I hurt her feelings and I know I do, but I can't help it. The more she tries to be nice the angrier I feel."
> **Holly, 16**

On the other hand, if you hate yourself all the time, it's likely to affect your behaviour and your actions in a negative way, and this often leads to some of the self-destructive behaviour explained above. Anger is also a direct result of self-hate – not just aggressive anger aimed at others but anger that is also directed at yourself.

Anger management is the best way to learn how to handle your angry feelings so that your anger doesn't hurt you or others (see Resources). The first step towards effective anger management is to understand the roots of your anger. Usually, angry outbursts are the result of factors such as frustration, rejection, failure and pressure. If you can learn to deal with these factors you'll then be able to manage your anger more effectively. Your goal isn't to never feel angry again (which, let's face it, is impossible) but to be able to express your anger in an acceptable way that isn't self-destructive or aggressive and violent towards others.

> "My teachers say I am too aggressive, but I can't help it, when someone winds me up I just snap. One girl laughed at me during netball the other day and I thought no one treats me like that, and went for her. My friends said I was out of order, and I probably did overreact but I can't stand people thinking I'm a no one."
>
> **Dionne, 15**

Body Image SOS

Are you up to your eyeballs with confidence, or scoring so low on the self-assurance scale that you're scraping the barrel? If you're like the majority of girls out there you're probably a mixture of the two: sometimes fired up with buckets of self-belief and sometimes crippled with self-doubt.

Body image fact: 94 per cent of girls under 18 wish they were more beautiful, and 1 in 4 would change everything about herself if given the chance. (Heat Group, Australia)

On these low days you may find that there is nothing you like about yourself. Your personality stinks, your body looks odd and, well, you probably hate everyone and are sure they hate you back. Feeling like this to a certain degree is normal, after all you're only human. But when you feel like this for weeks and months on end you've got a problem, because what you're doing is thinking yourself into a rut that's going to be almost impossible to climb out of.

Body image fact: 75 per cent of girls with low self-esteem report engaging in negative activities such as disordered eating and cutting (self-harm) and drinking when they feel bad about themselves.
(Dove, Real Girls, Real Pressure Report 2008)

While the process of puberty has a lot to answer for in feeling uncertain and unsettled, it's not the only factor that lowers your self-esteem and makes you feel full of self-loathing. Whether you realise it or not there are a number of ways our self-esteem and body image can get battered, and these all play an integral part in making us feel low about ourselves.

Body image fact: seven out of ten girls believe they are not good enough or don't measure up in some way. (Dove, Real Girls, Real Pressure Report 2008)

If you want to feel gorgeous inside and out, it's vital to understand not only why it's so important to have high self-esteem and a healthy body image but also what's affecting your self-esteem. So how's a girl to up her levels of self-esteem? Well, the first thing you have to look at is who and what is bringing you down.

The negative influences

Is it your friends, the clique of girls at school, the magazines you read or the things your family say to you that are dragging you down, or all of this and more? Only you can say, but this section can help you to look at some of the main factors that could be making you feel bad and it can show you what to do if you're falling prey to them.

What is self-esteem?

Self-esteem is about the big picture, not just how you feel about your looks, but about how you rate your personality traits, your intelligence, your skills and who you are as a person. As a result, self-esteem directly affects how you relate to others, what you feel you deserve in life and how you behave.

Bear in mind, though, that to increase your self-esteem you have to do more than just read about how to do it. It's important to put into practice what you learn about yourself and commit to changing your thinking and behaviour as you go. This way you can boost your self-confidence and feel better about yourself, not just become wise about why you have low self-esteem in the first place.

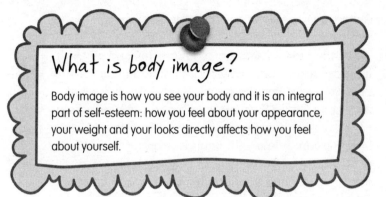

What is body image?

Body image is how you see your body and it is an integral part of self-esteem: how you feel about your appearance, your weight and your looks directly affects how you feel about yourself.

How do you feel about the real you?

Right here, right now, if you had to tell someone five things about yourself, how positive would those things be? Would you be complimentary and nice, or would you be hard on yourself and overly critical? Write it down and see what comes to mind. Now, looking at your list, answer the following:

- Have you been more positive, than negative?
- Is there a theme that stands out?
- Have you listed the five worst things about yourself or the five best?

Take a look at this example list by 12-year-old Megan:

- My nose is too big.
- I have nice hands.

- I am quite a good friend.
- I am too fat.
- I am bad tempered.

What can we tell about Megan from her list? Well, firstly, that she doesn't think much of the way she looks; she feels she's an OK person, but she's down on herself about her weight and her features. Overall, out of all the positive things she could have said about herself, all she can come up with is having nice hands. In reality, Megan is very funny, attractive and clever, but because she doesn't see these things, they don't appear on her list. So what does your list tell you about your feelings about yourself?

The real problem with being down on yourself is that if you can't see the good points or even acknowledge that you have them you will never believe that (1) you are a good person; and (2) other people truly like you for who you are.

Now try this exercise. On a scale of 1–5 (1 being the worst you feel and 5 being the best you feel), rate how you feel about the following aspects of yourself, by putting a circle around the appropriate number in each case. Bear in mind that this is a confidential list that you don't have to show anyone, and it works better if you can be as honest as possible:

Intelligence	1	2	3	4	5
Personality	1	2	3	4	5
Weight	1	2	3	4	5
Looks	1	2	3	4	5
Body shape	1	2	3	4	5
Being a daughter	1	2	3	4	5
Being a friend	1	2	3	4	5

The aim of this exercise is to see the areas of your life that are currently giving you the most self-esteem stress (see below for more on how to cope with these areas). It's a tough exercise in many ways, because we live in a society that doesn't encourage us to be complimentary about ourselves, so if you have scored low for fear of sounding big-headed or egotistic, go back and give the exercise another try.

Other signs of low self-esteem are when:

- You can't bear to look at your reflection in the mirror.
- You don't believe compliments that people give you.
- You feel you are fatter/uglier than everyone else you know.
- You don't believe anyone will ever want to go out with you.
- You're afraid to do new things for fear of people laughing at you.
- You feel unworthy compared to your friends.
- You feel you are letting down the people that you love.
- You constantly seek reassurance that you look OK.
- You're hard on yourself for not being perfect.
- You don't think you have anything to offer the world.
- You hate being the centre of attention (but secretly crave it).

Remember that good self-esteem is not about being big-headed, it's simply being honest about who you are and allowing yourself to feel good about the great aspects of yourself. This is very different from being a person who goes around constantly telling everyone how fantastic, amazing and attractive he or she is as a person. This kind of person doesn't have high esteem because what they are actually doing is seeking approval and attention, because they don't really believe these things about themselves.

Why it's important to build good self-esteem

Work on improving your self-esteem and you can say goodbye to all of the signs listed above, because a healthy self-esteem and body image will be your shield against the world. It may not help you to score a perfect 5 in all the areas in the exercise above, but it will help you to weather life when something hard happens, such as if you fail an exam or your best friend goes off with someone new, or you feel at odds with your body.

A small word of warning here: although I am talking about self-esteem as if it's the be-all and end-all that will forever improve your life, it's not a ticket to feeling happy all the time. For starters, no one feels happy all the time, but what having a good level of self-esteem will do is help you to feel buoyant when things are bad and stop you from the negative self-talk that keeps your focus firmly on the parts of yourself that you don't like.

A healthy self-esteem will also stop you from judging yourself (and others) harshly, and help you to be positive about the way you look. It will also help you to forgive yourself for the mistakes you make and to accept who you are as a person – with your good points, bad points and all the in-between points. Pretty good huh? So here's what may be bringing you down and what you can start doing about it.

The body image slammers – obsessing about your body shape

In an ideal world body shape wouldn't be an issue for anyone. We'd all be happy to live and let live, and understand that beauty comes in all shapes and sizes. Unfortunately, you don't need to be a brain surgeon to see that certain body types are applauded in society whereas others are condemned. This is why so many of us feel so bad about our bodies, feeling we just aren't measuring up and that it's all our own fault.

> "I hate the way I look. My legs are too short, my middle too fat. I want to go on a diet but my mum won't let me."
> **Sara 11**

Body fact: standards of beauty have become harder and harder to attain. The current media ideal of thinness is achievable by less than 5 per cent of women.

As Chapter One shows, body-shape changes at puberty are normal, but when it starts to happen, nearly everyone feels self-conscious about it. However, being self-conscious is one thing, and feeling disgusted about how you look and yearning for a drastically different body type is another, so try this quiz to see how you fare on the body-conscious scale.

Quiz: Are you too body-conscious?

For the following questions draw a circle around the answer that seems closest for you, then add up your scores at the end.

1 When you look at your body are you only able to see its flaws?
Yes
No

2 Do you feel having a great body is out of your reach?
Yes
No

3 Do you feel your life would be 100 per cent better if you had been given a taller/shorter/curvier/thinner body?
Yes
No

4 Does the perfect body exist?

Yes

No

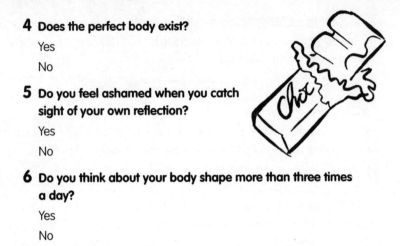

5 Do you feel ashamed when you catch sight of your own reflection?

Yes

No

6 Do you think about your body shape more than three times a day?

Yes

No

Scores

More than 5 yeses

You don't need me to tell you you're overly preoccupied with your body shape, because you know it and it's probably making you completely miserable. There is, however, a way out: try the techniques below and learn how to view your body size more realistically.

More than 3 yeses

You're on your way to being too body conscious. You need to look at what and who is feeding your body-shape obsession and view what you're seeing and hearing about bodies more realistically.

Fewer than 2 yeses

Congratulations, you're able to view your body in a healthy way, but make sure you stay that way by not falling prey to any of the factors below.

The truth is that we live in a world obsessed with glamour, weight and celebrities, and as a result the idea of what equals an attractive body has become incredibly small. It wasn't always this way; in decades gone by a curvy shape was more celebrated than a thin one, in another decade bigger breasts, longer legs and even more athletic women were the pinnacle of beauty. The point being, the lines of what's considered attractive in terms of body shape move constantly.

Body image fact: all research to date on body image shows that women are much more critical of their appearance than men and much less likely to admire what they see in the mirror. Up to eight out of ten women will be dissatisfied with their reflection, and more than half may see a distorted image. (Social Issues Research Centre)

If you have a fixation on your body shape, it's likely to be the result of what everyone around you is currently telling you equals being attractive, as well as what you're focusing on: magazines, celebrities and models (or your friends). It's also likely to be down to the experiences you have gone through; that is, what people have said about your body and said about their own, and so on. It's a negative spiral and one that can make you unhappy no matter what good stuff happens to you, which is why it's vital to look at what's driving your body-shape mania.

Problem 1: magazines

Magazines, especially ones that fixate on the shape of celebrities, as well as diets and how people look, can make you feel overly conscious about your own shape and unhappy with the way you look. They can also make you feel that everyone is long and thin (they're not) and that you can only be considered attractive if you look like them.

Solution 1: stop reading the magazines, or at least limit how often you read them. It's only by taking them out of your life that you'll realise what an effect they are having on you and your thought process. Try this exercise: read your regular magazines and afterwards write down three things you feel about your body.

Now avoid all magazines for a week and at the end of the week write down three things you feel about your body. Now compare lists. The first list is likely to be more negative than the first. This is because we are heavily influenced by what we read, so if you're constantly reading about women and their body shapes, this is where your focus will be.

Problem 2: TV programmes

Programmes and films can also make you believe that only a certain type of person can be successful and attractive, because shows aimed directly at teenagers tend to stick to an idealised body type and look rather than show a variety of shapes and sizes. This is why two major studies show that the amount of time you watch soaps, movies and TV shows is directly related to your degree of body dissatisfaction.

Solution 2: diversify what you watch so that you can see that TV does actually reflect all shapes, sizes and variations in attractiveness. Try watching different programmes, such as documentaries, real life and drama to get a more all-over view of what people look like. Better still, pay attention when you're out and about, and note that everyday people like you and me don't epitomise those who we see on TV because, in general, TV is about escapism, not realism.

Problem 3: your family

How your family (siblings and extended family) talk about body shape also contributes to how you view these issues and how you feel you measure up.

Solution 3: be willing to confront the way the female form is discussed in your home, pointing out how comments and attitudes make you feel about your own body. Bear in mind that much of what's said may be subconscious – in other words, your mum or dad doesn't realise how much emphasis they put on looking a certain way. This doesn't mean you can't discuss it but rather that you need to point it out as it's happening.

Problem 4: your mother

Is your mother overly critical about her own body? Is she always pointing out her body flaws and saying she wishes she were taller/bigger up top/smaller in the bottom? Studies show all these things can contribute towards you having a bad body image too.

Solution 4: talk to your mum about how she's making you feel about your own body, as it's unlikely she realises what she's saying, how much she says it or what messages you're picking up.

Problem 5: models

Wanting to be a model or look like a model, or constantly comparing yourself to a model's body is a good way to make yourself feel bad about your own body. Models are a breed apart, which is why they are models in the first place. You can scream, 'It's not FAIR!' all you like, but they are genetically predisposed to being naturally, tall, thin and lean. Which means that if you are short and curvy there is no way your body shape is ever going to match theirs, so stop comparing yourself. As a famous ad campaign once said, 'There are 3 billion women who don't look like supermodels and only 8 that do'.

Solution 5: studies show the average model is 10 per cent taller and weighs 23 per cent less than the average woman, so forget comparing body shapes. It's a game you'll never win.

The body image slammers – diets and dieting

It is estimated that the UK diet industry is worth one billion pounds a year – not surprising when you consider that we are a society obsessed with dieting, diet products, diet books and diet meals. Yet, despite all this, statistics show that diets don't work,

simply because they are not concerned with how you feel about yourself and why you're eating, but only with what you are eating.

Diets don't look at why you'd rather eat chips for lunch rather than a salad, and they do little to modify your eating choices for the long term, which means you spend the whole time on a diet fantasising about the food you really want. Once your diet is over you immediately go back to an old way of eating (and so regain any weight you may have lost).

> "I am always on a diet, because it's horrible being fat at school. Boys don't like you and if you eat normal lunches some girls look at me as if I am a pig so I try to pretend I am not hungry and skip eating."
>
> **Tia, 12**

How dieting damages your self-esteem

Diets and the unhealthy weight-loss strategies that go along with them, such as skipping meals, eating one food over all others and counting calories, play havoc with your self-esteem because all they do is make you fixate on what you're not – that is, not thin, not slim enough and not good enough. They also set in place unhealthy eating patterns for life and a negative way of thinking about your body, and weight.

Take a look at these facts:

- One in six women often skips meals to keep her weight down.
- One in four of us are trying to lose weight 'most of the time'.
- 62 per cent of teenage girls use unhealthy methods of weight control.

- 22 per cent of teenage girls admit to using diet pills, vomiting and laxatives.

The message that's lost within all the talk about diets is that there is a big difference between healthy dieting (dieting because you have weight to lose and need to get healthy by eating healthier meals) and unhealthy dieting (extreme dieting and extreme eating behaviours in order to reach an unrealistic body weight).

The only way to look good

Whereas there is a large amount of pressure to be slim and look good, it's important to realise that dieting is the worst way to lose weight and feel good about yourself. The only way to give yourself a healthy body that you'll be happy with for life is to exercise and eat a well-balanced and healthy diet that contains all the food groups: protein (meat, fish, eggs, tofu, nuts, beans and lentils), carbohydrates (pasta, rice and bread), fat (cheese and milk), vegetables and fruit (five portions a day). Foods which are unhealthy (sweets, cakes, biscuits, crisps and fast food) can be eaten in moderation; so that means, one of these things in a small portion, once a day (for more on this see Chapter Four).

Are you fixated with dieting?

If you're a diet addict, and always desperate to know how someone has dropped loads of weight, or eager to try anything that offers you a quick fix, the questions to ask yourself are:

1 **Do you really need to lose weight?** To find out, ask your doctor so that you can work out if this is something you need to do for health or if it's something you want to do because you feel it's a ticket to happiness.

2 **Are you dieting to keep up with friends?** You are five times more likely to diet if you have friends who diet. Although it can be hard to be the odd one out, bear in mind that friends should not dictate what you should or shouldn't be eating or what size you should be.

3 **Are you dieting because you feel being thinner** will make you more popular with your peers and boys? If so, question your belief. Thin doesn't necessarily mean nicer, or happier or more popular. And it definitely doesn't mean you'll be a girl inundated with dates.

4 **What is your definition of normal body weight** and is it in line with what others consider a normal body weight? In other words, is your view at odds with other people's? If so, you need to rethink your view and consider what it is based on and why.

The diet offenders

The worst kinds of diets are:

⭐ **Low-fat diets** – these are bad news when you're a teen because you need to eat a certain amount of fat for puberty and fertility to kick in.

⭐ **Low-calorie diets** – these are dangerous and will leave you feeling low in energy and depressed.

⭐ **Diets that restrict certain food groups**. A diet that requires you to say no to carbohydrates, such as bread or pasta, is unhealthy. You won't get the nutrients you need.

⭐ **Crash diets** – also known as miracle diets that promise a large weight loss in a short time, are unhealthy and dangerous to your health.

The body image slammers – your peer group

Your friends and classmates can have a large impact on how you feel about your body. Studies show that the more your friends diet and are a source of dieting information, the more likely you are to have low body image. Also, the more frequently you compare your body to those of others your age, the more weight and shape fixated you are likely to be.

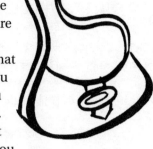

Even more interesting is the fact that studies show that the peer group you identify with can determine how you control your own eating habits. Researchers have been finding that there is a direct link between who you hang out with and your attitude to diet, weight and your body image.

- Girls identifying with sporty friends are less concerned about their own weight and less likely to try to control their weight, usually because their focus is on fitness.
- Girls identifying with a more artsy crowd are more concerned about their weight and appearance and more likely to be trying to lose weight.
- Girls who do not belong to any particular peer group are the most likely to use slimming strategies, usually as a way to fit in.

Although it can be hard to stand firm against what everyone else you know is doing, bear in mind that ultimately it's you who will always be the loser if you have unhealthy weight-loss strategies. If you feel you need to lose weight and you can't get the idea out of your head, the crucial thing to do is get your weight checked by a professional, such as a doctor or a state-registered dietician, or even a school nurse. Unlike your friends, these people are trained and will be able to tell you if your weight is in correlation to your height and age. If it's not, they can then advise you on your best course of action.

At the same time, talk to your friends about what's happening, highlighting how often you all talk about weight and your bodies. Consider whether you are fuelling each other's fears about being overweight? Then try to wean yourself off the subject by limiting daily body talk about it to five minutes or less.

The body image slammers – feeling you are fat

Believe it or not, it's not your weight but your perception of your size that counts when it comes to a bad body image. According to a study of 7,000 teenage girls, 'feeling fat' had a greater effect on self-esteem than a girl's actual weight.

Weight – it's an obsession

If you're someone who weighs herself three times a week or even three times a day, you are what is known as weight-obsessed, and you're sadly not alone. One survey of 2,000 girls found:

⭐ 60 per cent said they felt they would be happier if they lost weight.

⭐ 67 per cent thought they needed to lose weight.

⭐ 75 per cent thought thin girls were more popular with boys.

⭐ 50 per cent despaired that they would never look like their female role model.

(Bliss Survey 2004, UK)

The reality is that most girls worry that they are 'too fat'. Yes, even the girl you know who looks most like a model and even the friend who you'd most like to be. If you've said 'I'm fat', it's likely it happened on the bathroom scales and took place after weighing yourself with clothes on, then without clothes, then balancing on one leg and then holding on to something! The net result being horror at not making a magic thin number and a day/week/life of misery, where all you do is hate yourself for not being thin.

Yet the irony is that despite all the sensational headlines claiming we're a nation of fatties, only one in four teenage girls is classed as being overweight or obese. This means it's likely that you're in the 75 per cent of teenage girls who are just fine the way they are (and even if you're not, it's not the end of the world, because you can change things – more on that later). What's really bad news, though, is not how much you weigh but how obsessed you are with being fat.

To see how you fare on the weight-obsessed scale try this quick quiz.

Quiz: How weight-obsessed are you?

For the following questions draw a circle around the answer that seems closest for you, then add up your scores at the end.

1 Is how positive or negative you feel about the day dependent on how 'fat' you feel?

Yes

No

2 Are you secretly pleased when you walk into a room and see someone fatter than you in there?

Yes

No

3 Do you often imagine people are talking about your weight?

Yes

No

4 Do you feel ashamed of your size?

Yes

No

5 Do you feel your life would be 100 times better if you weighed less?

Yes

No

6 Are you addicted to reading about how celebrities lose weight?
Yes
No

Scores

3 or more yeses
You're weight-obsessed.

2 yeses
Be careful, you're on the borderline of being weight-obsessed.

1 yes
You're fine just the way you are.

Changing your mindset

If you're miserable defining yourself by your weight, here's how to change the record and start being less obsessed about fat.

- Instead of focusing on what you're not, ask yourself, 'What can I do right now to be happier?' You can't alter your weight in five minutes, but you can change your mindset by literally deciding to be positive about yourself.

- Stop the negative fat talk. Every time you feel fat, pay attention to what you are saying to yourself and balance it up by saying (or thinking) something positive for every negative. If you can't find a positive, stop listing the negatives.

- Get weight scales into perspective. All they do is measure what you weigh at a given point in time. They don't take into account weight fluctuations caused by periods or puberty, or even how much you've been drinking or sweating in a day.

- How you look today isn't a predictor of how you'll look tomorrow. Give your body time to morph into its perfect shape, and while it's happening give yourself a much deserved weight break.

When you are overweight

Studies show there is a definite correlation between low self-esteem and being overweight. It's hardly surprising when you think of how overweight people are made to feel and the associations we have about being fat. However, being fat doesn't have to mean being unhappy, miserable and depressed.

Research shows that overweight teenagers who have the lowest self-esteem have parents or friends who tease or bully them about their weight problems and may also be bullied at school. Which means that if you feel bad about yourself you first have to do something about who is making you feel bad. Seek help for bullying at school (see below) and tell your parents how their comments make you feel about yourself.

If you know for sure that you are overweight and you want to do something about it, you need to work out why you overeat. For people who are overweight there is more to it than unhealthy eating habits, and in most cases there is an emotional component to eating. Perhaps you feel lonely, or unhappy, or you hate yourself or feel empty inside; food then fills this gap and makes you feel better or becomes your best friend. This is comfort eating, and the problem with it is that it leads to the following vicious cycle:

You feel sad or low, so you eat. You then feel bad for eating, and so feel even more low and sad. You then turn to food and eat again – and feel sad and low again.

By comparison, doing something positive about your weight and getting healthy will help set in motion a better cycle where you feel good about your achievements, and so your self-esteem rises, encouraging you to stay healthy.

Even if you feel desperate and beyond help, remember that there are people who can help you to lose weight, such as dieticians and your doctor. There are also plenty of organisations that specialise in helping teenagers with weight problems and low self-esteem (see Resources). However, it's also important to live in the present and to find ways to feel good about yourself now. Being overweight doesn't mean having to be unhappy. Try to:

1. Play to your strengths

Success is a massive self-esteem booster, so figure out what some of your strengths are and pursue activities related to that. Are you a good listener? Could you become a teen mentor? If you are committed to a cause, why not volunteer your time for that and see what impact you can have.

2. Take healthy risks

Try some new physical activities to show yourself that you can do things in an area that you may not have thought about before. It doesn't have to be sport. Buy a fitness DVD and do it in your bedroom, learn to dance or simply go for a walk every day.

3. Find your talents

Have you let your weight stop you from trying new things and participating in life? If so, find out what you're good at by making yourself try new things. It doesn't have to be physical if you feel that's too painful; try music, an art class, writing or photography – basically something that is about using your creative mind and not just focusing on your weight.

4. Find people who can support you

Having a strong social support structure is important no matter what you weigh. Open up and talk to friends, relatives and teachers, and even online forums (though obviously be cautious about what information you give out online and use reputable forums and networking sites only), which can provide you with the kind of emotional support that you (and everyone else) needs to get through the hard parts of life.

5. Be nice to yourself

Just because you're overweight it doesn't mean you have to punish yourself or be mean to yourself, or take abuse from other people – and this includes teasing. Don't just laugh off hurtful comments; tell people how it makes you feel and that you don't

want them to do it. Take action against
bullying by telling someone what's going
on (see Resources) and never ever feel
you deserve to be treated badly just
because you're overweight.

6. Dress for your shape

Just because you're bigger than your
friends doesn't mean that you can't wear nice
clothes. Hiding your body away is part of hiding your
personality away, so dress for your shape (even if you don't like it
much), for more on this see Chapter Four. This means wearing
clothes that fit, standing tall and holding your head up high so
that people don't read you as a person who is ashamed of
who she is.

7. Realise that your weight doesn't define you

What you weigh doesn't define who you are as a person. Just
because you're overweight doesn't mean that you are the things
society associates with being fat – and it doesn't mean you can't
be happy, fall in love or be successful. There are plenty of people
who don't conform to society's idea of 'attractive' who are
successful and happy. The key is to be happy with the weight you
are, and if you're not, do something about it (see below).

8. Do something positive about your weight

It's not what you weigh but staying where you are and not taking
action that can make you feel helpless and horrible about
yourself. To help yourself do something positive, whether that's
participating more in life, taking action against bullies or
increasing exercise and healthy eating in your life. Better still,
talk to a counsellor or doctor about your weight and let them
help you find strategies to cope.

9. Ignore the size-zero and obesity debate

Size zero is a women's clothing size in the US equivalent to a UK
size 4, with a waist measurement of 58cm (23in) (the average
girth of an eight-year-old girl). It is being sold to us all as the

ultimate way to look good. At the same time we are also being given obsessive messages about obesity and how bad it is to be fat.

The reality is that less than 1 per cent of the celebrities you see are 'naturally' a size zero. Most super-thin celebrities are on a permanent diet, and eating so little they are constantly hungry. As for obesity, it is a problem, but one that can be solved by healthy eating and daily activity. It's not something to be embarrassed about, feared or something that will just sneak up on you.

10. See yourself as a whole person

Think of yourself as a person who's not defined by their weight. Whatever you weigh you are also someone's friend, someone's daughter, and probably someone's shoulder to lean on. You're also likely to be smart, funny and talented, and just as worthy as everyone else out there. Seeing yourself as a whole person with a surplus of things to offer can improve your self-esteem and help you to be more positive about yourself and your life.

The body image slammers – eating disorders

Eating disorders such as anorexia nervosa and bulimia affect one in 100 girls, and although there is no single cause for an eating disorder, what is known is that girls with eating disorders don't feel good about themselves on the inside. This makes them try to change the outside by controlling what they eat and how they grow (or, in the case of anorexia, how they don't grow).

Studies show that being involved in certain activities, such as ballet and modelling, can also make it more likely that you may develop an eating disorder, because in these interests, bodies are viewed closely, and being thin or slim is promoted above everything else.

When food becomes the enemy

If you or a friend is currently indulging in extreme weight-loss strategies be aware of the following, as they are signs that an eating problem may be brewing:

1 Skipping meals.

2 Eating alone so that no one can see you eat.

3 Making yourself sick or taking laxatives (which by the way doesn't help you to lose weight) when you eat 'bad' foods.

4 Exercising when you eat too much.

5 Feeling in control when you don't eat.

6 Feeling you're fat when everyone around you expresses the opposite opinion.

7 Having a fat phobia, where you feel the world would end if you gained weight.

8 Having a distorted body image: thinking you're much fatter and bigger than you actually are.

9 Developing strange eating habits such as: cutting your food into tiny portions and pushing it around your plate.

10 Feeling depressed and isolated.

What is anorexia?

Anorexia is an eating disorder where a person is so afraid of becoming fat that she (or he) refuses to eat. Anorexics have a strong internal voice that makes them feel bad about eating, but at the same time they are obsessed with food and calories as well as exercising obsessively to burn off calories. The frightening aspect of anorexia is that it's life threatening, because no matter how thin people with anorexia become, they keep thinking they are fat and can starve themselves to death.

What is bulimia?

Bulimia is an eating disorder whereby sufferers binge and purge (make themselves sick, or take laxatives to hurry it through their system) to control their weight. This means a bulimic may eat a large meal, then secretly get rid of it by being sick or taking laxatives. Like anorexics, girls who have bulimia feel depressed and helpless, bulimia also depletes the body of essential nutrients and can affect heart and kidney function.

Break free from an eating disorder

If you suspect you or someone you know has an eating disorder, seek help from your family or through professional services (see Resources for experts who can help), because an eating disorder does not go away on its own. However, with the right help you can recover and go on to lead a normal life where food and weight isn't your primary focus.

How to improve your body image

Who do you want to look like? Can you picture this person in your mind? Is she someone you go to school with? A normal girl like you, the same age and the same build? Or does she happen to be famous? Is she taller, thinner, longer and leaner than you? Does she epitomise the kind of life you secretly crave? If so, you're not alone. It's normal to want to look like someone else (and even be someone else, like a model or actress), especially during puberty when you feel as if you don't fit in. However, in order to get your body image into perspective, it's important to make the distinction between reality and fantasy; that is, between what's possible and what's impossible for the body you have been given. This means that you have to accept your personal body facts: how tall and lean you will or won't be is mostly determined by your genes and not by what you eat and how much you exercise.

> "I want to feel good about myself; I really do, but what's the point in saying I am gorgeous when it's the last thing I feel."
> **Carly, 14**

We're not all made the same

Models, for example, are known as 'ectomorphs': people who are generally tall and thin, and have long arms and legs. Ectomorphs have difficulty gaining weight and muscle no matter how much they eat or how hard they weight train (yes, it's totally unfair, but that's life). They have the body type you tend to see in ballet dancers, runway models, long-distance runners and some athletes – and only 5 per cent of the population has this type of body.

By comparison, the rest of the population are either meso-morphs or endomorphs, or a mixture of the two. Mesomorphs are generally muscular and short with stocky arms and legs. These people are strong and may find it difficult to lose weight.

Endomorphs are generally shaped like apples or pears and carry more body fat than ectomorphs and mesomorphs. Their bodies resist losing weight and body fat, and as a result are better able to handle long periods of starvation and famine (which was a benefit to our ancestors).

Make the most of what you have

To improve your body image you have to work with what you've been given. So, accept that you can't change your body type; you can't be taller or shorter than you are genetically programmed to be. Of course, you can influence your weight, but if you are 1.5m (5ft 1in), no amount of not eating is going to turn you into a 1.77m (5ft 10in) model. (In fact, all it will do is delay your growth spurt in terms of height.)

The above body shapes don't mean that you are predestined to be fat or muscular but that you are naturally going to be a bit curvier than the ectomorphs you see in the media. Which is why it pays to be flexible with your thinking if you want to have a healthy body image. This means you need to be realistic about your body shape and be able to see the good in yourself as well as the bad. To do this, limit what's known as overcritical thinking and work on replacing each negative thought with a positive one every time you talk badly to yourself. Try to:

1 Talk to yourself as an encouraging best friend, rather than your own personal critic.

2 Every day, verbally appreciate the things you like about your own body (you probably do the opposite, so this is not as weird as it sounds).

3 Look at your beliefs and attitudes about the female body. Where have these come from and how true are they when you look at them objectively?

4 Consider whether you are around people who always talk negatively about their bodies? If so, does this make you look more closely at your own flaws and then talk about them more freely? If so, you need to limit this kind of conversation.

5 Stop blaming your body for everything that is wrong in your life.

Next, get friendly with your mirror image. All the research to date on body image shows that women are much more critical of their appearance than men, and much less likely to admire what they see in the mirror. Up to eight out of ten women will be dissatisfied with their reflection, and more than half may see a distorted image (they see themselves as uglier and bigger than they are).

Your mirror image

Try to:

1 View yourself from head to toe at least once a day.

2 Get used to seeing yourself naked, it's not as scary as you think it is and it will help you to connect with what your body really looks like.

3 Be aware of the images you look at and your own idea of what is a 'beautiful' body. Are these images realistic?

4 Dress for the shape you are right now (for more on this see Chapter Four), rather than dressing to hide and cover up, so you really make the most of who you are.

5 Like what you see in the mirror. Every time you look in the mirror, find three things you like about yourself and say them out loud.

So, think about this, when was the last time you looked at yourself in the mirror, full on from head to toe? If you have a problem with your body image, it's likely to have been quite a while ago. What people with a low self-esteem tend to do is focus on their body in parts but not as a whole. For example, when they look in the mirror they see themselves in compartments, such as: my hair is good, my face is OK, my body is awful, my arms look great, my legs are too fat, and so on. To accept your body image it's essential to look at yourself as a whole person.

> "My friends say I am not fat, but when I look in the mirror I see it. My legs are huge and my bottom really sticks out. I think they are being nice, and actually they can see it too."
> **Ella, 12**

Black and white

Finally, identify your negative thinking patterns. These are the extreme thoughts that feed our beliefs that we are unattractive, such as:

- **'If I am not a size 10, I must be fat'** – this is what's known as black-and-white thinking. It's irrational because anything above size 10 is not fat, plus if you want to feel good about yourself you can't just think of your body in terms of good/bad, fat/thin and attractive/unattractive. Consider all the grey areas in between.

- **'Boys only like thin girls'** – this is a generalisation and, like all generalisations, it's not true. Couples literally come in all shapes and sizes, and being thin doesn't make you more or less likely to be asked out. Generalisations like this make you feel as if you're being honest and rational when in fact you're doing the opposite. (And consider what other generalisations you might be making about weight, being fat and your body.)

- **'Boys don't ask me out because I am fat'** – this is a thought process whereby you blame your body for everything bad in your life. (Rationally, how can this be true? Weight has nothing to do with intellect, skills or how good a person you are.) The reality is that a boy may not have asked you out because he doesn't want a girlfriend, or already has one, or has other things on his mind.

- **'Even if I lost weight, I'd be ugly'** – this is negative and distorted thinking. Telling yourself that you're a hopeless case that can't be helped because no matter what you do something will always be wrong with you means you are putting yourself in a lose–lose situation every time.

Move forward by thinking about more than your body

Whatever you choose to do to improve your body image, it's vital that you don't make your body into an all-consuming project that feeds your fears and makes every day a living nightmare. To have a healthy body image and buckets of self-esteem it's important to work on developing interests and talents that play to your strengths and don't just focus on how you look. Try this hourly, daily, weekly and monthly exercise to help yourself along.

Exercise

1 For one whole hour each day, don't let yourself think/worry/fret/ agonise about your looks or weight, and every time you feel your mind drifting that way pull yourself back into focusing on someone else: a friend in need; your mum or your best friend. Practising being more externally focused instead of internally focused helps start to put your fears into perspective.

2 For one whole day, challenge yourself to do three things that you'd usually avoid. Whether it's speaking up in class, standing up for yourself with friends or making yourself face one fear. Your mind will try to step in and give you excuses to avoid doing it or reasons why you shouldn't try, but fight to override your anxiety, as this is the way to build confidence in yourself.

3 For one week, take all compliments given to you with a simple 'Thank you'. Then, instead of throwing them aside, thinking people are just being nice to you and forgetting about them, write them down and remember them (in the same way you remember all the put-downs you have ever been given). Then, the next time you feel bad, read through them and remember what other people think of you. Also, bear in mind that if you're given the same compliment more than once it's a cue for you to start believing in it.

4 Over the next four weeks, take up, or start participating in, a sport. It doesn't have to be team related, try signing up for a dance class, jogging or just making yourself go to every PE class at school. As I mentioned in Chapter One, research shows that girls who participate in sport have a more positive body image than those who do not. So, this is about focusing your mind on the external things that your body can achieve to build confidence in yourself.

The beauty image slammers – your idea of beauty

Body image fact: by the time the average girl is 12 years old, she will have been exposed to more than 77,000 advertisements.
(Dove, Onslaught Campaign)

The pressure to be pretty begins for most of us as soon as we are born. Ask your mum what people used to say about you as a baby or toddler and it's likely you were complimented for being cute, pretty and beautiful as opposed to strong and brave (which tend to be boy compliments). As a result, as girls we learn pretty quickly that it's our looks that get us attention and approval from others, even when we know this shouldn't be the case and that we are a lot more than that. Unfortunately, it's a fact that's then slammed home to us by the beauty industry and the endless attention given to 'beautiful, females' whether they are girls in your class, or celebrities, models and actresses, who make the definition for being beautiful feel very small and rigid.

As a result, as a girl you are more likely to be self-critical about your looks than a boy is about his. Also, the more you are exposed to images of female beauty the more it appears that exceptional good looks are normal and that anything short of perfection seems abnormal and ugly, so you are more likely to hate your looks.

What's more, the definition of what it means to be beautiful keeps changing. Twenty-five years ago the top models and actresses weighed only 8 per cent less than the average woman; now they weigh 23 per cent less, which makes the current beauty ideal in terms of weight, height, shape and facial characteristics achievable by less than 1 per cent of the population. And that, in a nutshell, is the problem with letting others dictate what being beautiful should mean. It puts you at the mercy of fashion's fickle eye and keeps you tied to a very rigid idea of what it means to be beautiful.

> "The pictures in magazines make me feel horrible because I know that even if I had plastic surgery I could never look that good."
> **Chloe, 12**

Quiz: How beautiful do you feel?

For the following questions draw a circle around the answer that seems closest for you, then add up your scores at the end.

1 **When you compare yourself to other girls, do you always feel less attractive?**

Yes

No

2 **Is the most beautiful woman you can think of someone famous or well known?**

Yes

No

3 Do you secretly feel that plastic surgery is the answer to your problems?

Yes

No

4 If someone tells you you're beautiful, do you automatically think they are just being nice?

Yes

No

5 When you look in the mirror, do you immediately feel depressed?

Yes

No

6 Can you name three things about your look that you feel are more than OK?

Yes

No

Scores

More than 5 yeses

You have a negative self-image and currently don't feel you are beautiful or attractive in any way. Don't worry, you're not alone, and there are plenty of things you can do to feel better about yourself – see below for more on this.

More than 3 yeses

You have a wavering self-image, some days you feel on top of the world and on other days you're at the bottom of the barrel. You need to work on your resilience – that's your ability to recover from setbacks and life's harder moments. Read on to find out how.

More than 2 yeses

Well done! You may have your off-days but on the whole you feel good about your looks. It means you have a good level of self-esteem and are able to stand firm against outside pressures to conform.

So, what's a girl to do?

If you want to feel beautiful, the first thing to recognise is what's affecting your view of beauty and stopping you from feeling beautiful. One of the main things that may affect your thinking is what you see every day. That's the millions of advertising images that are constantly telling us to get rid of our imperfections: buy this, do that, eat this and we're told we'll have softer, firmer, younger, brighter, clearer, skin, hair, nails, teeth, and so on. And what do these messages ultimately tell us?

- That we're not good enough the way we are.
- That if we look bad it's our fault.
- If we try we can improve our looks.
- That to look beautiful we have to spend time and money on ourselves.
- That imperfections are bad.

What advertising doesn't tell us is that the pictures we see of perfect, beautiful women advertising products aren't how these models really look. No product or amount of trying will ever make you look this way. If you don't believe me, look closely at the face of a woman on a magazine cover and consider if in your whole life you have ever seen a woman with a face that perfect? A woman on a magazine cover is likely to have no lines, no blemishes, no spots, no hair out of place and no laughter lines, because all those things are zapped out using digital computer techniques.

The other thing to remember is that we focus on what we're surrounded by, so if you watch a lot of TV, read magazines and spend a lot of time discussing beauty products, make-up and your beauty flaws with your friends, that's where your focus will be. To help yourself get your looks into perspective, it's important to balance up what you're seeing with real life:

- **Beauty is in the eye of the beholder**. If you look at yourself with deeply critical eyes, that is all you will see. To see your good points, it's essential first to acknowledge that there are beautiful parts to yourself. This means being less critical and more forgiving. So what if your eyes aren't big enough? Are they a great colour/shape or do they have a fantastic twinkle when you smile?

- **What images of real beauty are there around you?** Think of three beautiful women of different ages that you know and consider what makes them beautiful. Is it their attitude, their look, or the way they make the most of themselves? If you can't find any real examples, think about why this is the case. Only seeing beauty in famous people shows that your idea of what is beautiful is way too narrow and probably a tad unrealistic. So, you need to widen your view. Think of this: what makes your best friend beautiful? And your mum? And your friends?

- **What is beautiful?** Get together with your mum and your best friend and come up with a list of beautiful women. Now compare lists and see how your views of beauty differ. The idea with this exercise is to see that we all find different things beautiful and no one is right and no one is wrong.

- **Think about your beauty ideal.** We all have one person who we think is beautiful above all others and it's fine to have that person in mind when we think of being beautiful. However, this person shouldn't be your only definition of beauty. Being attractive encompasses a large number of things. The narrower your field of vision, the harder it will be for you to feel beautiful.

The beauty image slammers – the beauty industry

Before you hit puberty, there is very little reason to pay attention to what the beauty industry is selling you because, let's face it, you don't have anything to worry about. Your hair is unlikely to be greasy/dry, your skin isn't covered with pimples and you're definitely not emitting any bodily odours. Of course, puberty changes all that. Suddenly you're going to be targeted by advertising, which is going to feed your beauty anxieties and tempt you to buy all kinds of products by telling you that you *need* to buy, X, Y and Z, if you want to look and feel beautiful.

Now, advertising isn't the big bad wolf, because no one can make you buy something you don't want or aren't interested in. However, if your focus is on a particular area of yourself – such as your skin – adverts can make you more conscious and worried about yourself. So, here are the advertising beauty myths that are worth standing firm against:

Flawless skin products

Having flawless skin is a myth unless you're a baby, and then of course your skin is going to be super-soft and blemish-free. Other than that it isn't going to be flawless, because skin is our body's protective layer, and it naturally gets battered by everything, from the wind and cold weather to the hot weather, and so it is affected by everything we have done up until now. That's not a reason to feel depressed, though, because, in the grand scheme of things, having flawless skin is not essential.

However, suddenly having spotty skin, lots of blackheads and acne scars is something that can make you feel horribly self-conscious, and pull you into the beauty trap of wanting perfect skin. The truth here is that spots and blackheads are caused by puberty and not by what you do or don't wash your face with. Flawless skin can't be achieved with exfoliators, miracle spot potions and an over-zealous beauty regime. The only way to rid your face of spots is to try over the counter medication for spots (ask your pharmacist) or see your doctor for antibiotics (see Chapter One for more on this) that fight the reasons behind acne occurring.

As for acne scars, don't be pulled into buying products that tell you they can change your skin tone. Your doctor can also treat acne scars, but only once your acne is on the wane (during late puberty). This may seem ages to wait, but treatment is usually laser resurfacing, which removes the damaged top layer of skin and tightens the middle layer, leaving the skin smoother.

Stretch-mark creams

Although most of the miracle stretch-mark creams say they contain vitamins to repair the skin, the reality is that the vitamins are in such low doses (because of regulations over what cosmetics can contain) that they will not do anything. These creams feed on your fears about being imperfect when you don't have to worry, because most people have stretch marks and forget they even have them.

Cellulite cream

There is a huge debate about whether cellulite even exists, but as a teenage girl it shouldn't even be on your radar. However, thanks to the endless talk around the subject and the endless pictures of celebrities being slated for having dimply bottoms and thighs, you may find yourself being worried about it. So here is what you need to know:

- The current thinking is that cellulite is simply fat depositing in certain areas of the body in a different way so that it ends up looking dimply. This is why some very slim and athletic women get it and other women don't. There is also a genetic factor to it, so you may have inherited cellulite, which means a cream isn't going to make it go away.

- As the effect is going on below the skin, no miracle cream can penetrate your skin to affect what's going on. So, don't be tempted to buy anything that promises to eliminate the effect of cellulite. What's more, don't even focus on what your thigh/bottom may or may not be doing. It's hugely unlikely you have cellulite in any case!

Bouncy hair

Hair adverts are the worst when it comes to selling a distorted view of what hair can look like. If you've always craved the bouncy, thick, dazzling hair you see in adverts, be aware that this isn't created by the hair product you're seeing, but by hours of work by a hairdresser, plus hair colour (which adds texture and makes hair look thicker) and hair extensions (which make hair look longer and thicker) and studio lights (which give hair it's deep colour and shine). All in all, this means you're being sold a vision of perfect hair that isn't attainable for everyday life.

Perfect white teeth

Our teeth aren't made to be perfectly white, even and shiny. Teeth that look like this are likely to be veneers (wafer-thin shells of porcelain that are bonded onto the front of teeth to create a cosmetic improvement) and have been whitened with a bleaching process. Normal teeth tend to be less than white and not so even. So, don't be fooled into buying expensive products that promise to give you a Hollywood smile, because the only way to get this is via cosmetic dentistry.

Cosmetic and plastic surgery

Teenage cosmetic surgery is on the increase, thanks to the way some cosmetic procedures have become associated with normal everyday beauty, which is why recently several doctors' groups have cautioned teenagers against resorting to major surgery as a quick fix for self-esteem. Apart from it being a bad idea before your body has fully stopped growing, the truth no one ever tells you is that surgery isn't a solution to low self-esteem and a bad body image.

Surgery doesn't work; simply because having bigger/smaller breasts, less fat, a smoother face and smaller nose won't suddenly bring you popularity or self-belief or even inner beauty. Which is why it's helpful to know that one major study found body-image satisfaction occurs not with plastic surgery but with age. With image dissatisfaction, rates are the highest when you are 11 years and the lowest when you reach age 18 years.

How to improve your beauty image

Improving how you feel about your looks is part of improving your overall body image and an important aspect of making yourself feel gorgeous inside and out. Whereas the above sections can show you what eats away at your beauty confidence, it's also important to acknowledge what you're doing to yourself. First of all you need to know how playing the comparison game can make you feel about your looks.

Although it's a totally normal part of teenage life to compare yourself to other girls and your friends, always rating yourself is a negative game to play, because in most instances you are going to come out badly. Think of it this way: you're on your way out to a party, you spend ages getting dressed up and feel great. You walk into a room, check out your friends and suddenly feel deflated about yourself, because in your mind how you look is not as stylish, attractive, grown up or gorgeous as them. As a result, your confidence instantly drops and you no longer feel good; in fact all you want to do is go home and hide in your room.

This is what comparing yourself to others does. So, if you're going to indulge in it, try to:

1 **Keep your comparisons in perspective**. For instance, X looks better in jeans than you because she's taller than you, but perhaps you look better in tops than she does.

2 **Top up your confidence**. If you can instantly make yourself feel bad, you have the power to make yourself feel instantly good. A good way to do this is to think of a time you felt good about yourself when you felt really strong and confident. Bring this to mind and let it fill you with a surge of confidence.

3 **Think outside yourself**. Worrying constantly about how you look stops you from having fun. If you feel yourself agonising over what you look like, take a deep breath and immediately make yourself

focus on three things that have nothing to do with your looks; for example, the music, what's happening on the other side of the room, and if there is anyone around that you want to chat to.

4 **Stop worrying about what others think of you**. The truth is that they are all too busy worrying about what people think of them – meaning, no one is thinking about you. It sounds harsh but it's a very freeing realisation.

Beware of the makeovers

Next, be aware of what you're watching on TV. Makeover shows literally used to be about making over people with new clothes and new make-up, but these days they have taken it a bit further with certain shows focusing on surgical makeovers in order to 'improve' someone. Such programmes make it difficult to see what constitutes a 'normal' appearance. If you watch these shows, be aware of the following:

- Radical and major surgery is not the answer to better self-esteem and feeling beautiful. In fact, many of these contestants have crippling low self-esteem that isn't helped by being made over on these shows.

- Keep what you're seeing in perspective. Being beautiful isn't about looking perfect and having perfect features. Beauty is a much deeper concept that encompasses more than looks and perfection.

- We use the attitudes of others (that's people we know and the media) to shape our own judgement about what is attractive and beautiful. However, be aware that if you find someone beautiful and no one else does, it doesn't mean your definition is wrong and they are right. Beauty is, after all, in the eye of the beholder.

- Finally, feeling that you are ugly because you're not beautiful like your favourite celebrity or your friends is ridiculous. The reality is that you don't have to match up to anyone else to look or feel beautiful. If you feel that you are ugly, it's because you're giving yourself a hard time and ignoring the aspects of yourself that are wonderful and good. Spend more time thinking about what makes you beautiful and less time thinking about what doesn't and you'll find a miraculous thing happening: your body image and self-esteem will start to rise and rise, and one day you really will wake up feeling gorgeous.

Chapter
Three

Gorgeous in the Real World

> "No one can make you feel inferior
> without your permission."
> **Eleanor Roosevelt**

How do you feel you measure up in the real world? Are you a popular girl who has the world at her feet? Or do you feel like an outsider who doesn't quite fit in, or someone who constantly struggles to fit in but only ends up following the crowd and hating herself?

Self-esteem fact: seven in ten teenage girls don't feel they measure up.
(Dove Self-esteem Fund Survey)

Do you love your friends to death, or do they wind you up and get you down, act mean and make you feel like a failure? And what about your family – are they the rock you lean on and the people you count on, or do they make you feel bad about yourself and unsure about the world without even realising they are doing it?

"Some days I'll wake up feeling full of confidence and go to breakfast to hear my mum ask what's up with my hair and warn me to watch what I am eating. In just a few minutes she makes me feel horrible about myself."

Becky, 14

This section is all about your family and friends, because boosting your self-esteem is about more than looking at your reflection in the mirror, but about working on feeling good from the inside. It's also about looking at why you're so hard on yourself, discovering how other people can have a powerful effect on how you feel, and then working out what to do about it.

This means you can't improve your self-esteem without looking at the people who directly influence your life – that's your friends, your parents, boys and even your own responses to the world. It's not about blaming others for how you feel or making your parents and friends responsible for your self-esteem and confidence issues. It's about working out why you put up with what you do, what other people's issues are, and how to develop a strong sense of self so that you can cope with what the world throws at you.

Dealing with best friends, cliques and enemies

If all you want is to be like the popular girls in your class, then you're not alone. It's natural at any age to want to identify with your peers and feel accepted and approved of by the people around you, especially the powerful ones who seem to have all the control. However, this has its problems, because it ends up giving our friends and the people we know a lot of power when it comes to influencing how we feel about ourselves and our bodies.

If you have good friends, they will hopefully bolster you, make you feel good and reassure you when you feel down. Unfortunately, no matter how good your friends are, you are bound to come across girls (and even some family members and boys) who seem to do the opposite of this. These girls spread mean things about you, pretend to be your friend and then act the opposite way, and you might also have 'friends' who bully and try to control you or even exclude you and do their best to make you feel bad.

For this reason navigating the world of friendships, and especially school cliques, is hard, and at times it can feel impossible, especially when you're lacking in self-esteem. Yet the important thing to realise is that you're not alone. Just take a look at the following quotes from girls talking about their problems with friends.

"Recently my best friend has been going off with this other girl and emailing me with horrid comments, which makes me feel small."

Jessica, 13

"Two friends of mine moved forms and another friend said to me, 'It must be harder for you than for Charlotte and Emma.' And when I asked why, she said, 'Well, because they're really popular but you're not.' That left my self-esteem quite bashed!"

Lauren, 13

"A few weeks ago everyone got asked to this girl's party and I didn't. I tried to pretend it didn't matter, but it really hurt. She even invited my best friend right in front of me."

Sophie, 12

"At lunch the other day my best friend Molly said, 'Do you mind being fat?' I had to try really hard not to cry. I can't believe she was so mean; we've been friends since we were seven years old."

Charlotte, 12

Self-esteem fact: 50 per cent of teenage girls report that they engage in negative activity, such as bullying, gossiping and cutting (self-harm), when they feel bad about themselves. (Dove Self-esteem Fund Survey)

As hard as all the situations above are, there are ways to deal with them and ways that not only build self-esteem but also ensure that you aren't at the mercy of other people's mean behaviour. Much of this is to do with improving what's known as your social competence. That's the social, and emotional skills that enable you to understand what's behind someone else's bad behaviour. Understand this and you will be able to:

• See someone's real motives.
• Feel fine even if someone is trying to bring you down.
• Know what to do when friendships fall apart.
• Know what to do when you're being bullied.
• Know how to get rid of a bad friend.

- Be aware of how to handle cliques.
- Stand up for yourself, even if you feel scared.

A good starting place is to work out what kind of friend you are, as it's this that can tell you a lot about your current level of self-esteem, and also the way you let your friends treat you and the way you treat your friends.

Quiz: What kind of friend are you?

For the following questions tick the answer that seems closest for you, then add up your scores at the end:

1 You're having a party, what's your biggest fear?
  a. That you'll have to invite everyone in your class. (0)
  b. That people won't come. (5)
  c. That your party will be bad and everyone will gossip about you. (10)

2 A friend wakes you up with a boyfriend crisis at 11.00pm. You:
  a. Say it's no problem. (5)
  b. Tell her you're sleeping and hang up. (0)
  c. Feel grateful that she's chosen to call you. (10)

3 Your friends would describe you as:
  a. Popular and pretty. (0)
  b. A good listener and always there for them. (10)
  c. A bit of an outsider. (5)

4 In terms of gossip, are you the one who:
  a. Spreads it. (0)
  b. Listens to it. (10)
  c. Is the subject of it. (5)

5 When a friend makes you feel bad about yourself, you:
  a. Ignore it. (5)
  b. Tell them you're no longer friends. (0)
  c. Pretend it didn't happen. (10)

Scores

0–10 Ms Popularity

You are Ms Popularity and probably the head of a small clique of girls. You feel powerful because of your popularity, but in reality you feel afraid of letting anyone see the real you, and, as a result, you tend to try to control girls if you don't get your way.

15–25 The Outsider

You try to be true to yourself and, as a result, you sometimes feel like the outsider or the person people talk about. Your sense of self is stronger than most other girls, so rest assured you're on the right track.

30–50 The People Pleaser

You work hard to make people like you, allowing them to lean on you and take advantage of your nice qualities, but as a result you're unlikely to confront a friend who has hurt you or stand firm against a group of friends you believe are behaving badly.

Surviving cliques

Cliques are another name for a group of girls that are usually powerful in your school. Maybe they are the pretty girls, the popular girls or the girls who just know how to control other girls. Cliques tend to be exclusive in that the girls within the clique stick together and get their kicks from excluding other girls and making them feel (in a variety of ways) that they are not good enough to be with them.

If you're on the outside of a clique trying to get in, questions to ask yourself are:

1 Why are you eager to belong? Are you looking for approval from the popular girls, if so why?
2 Do you feel life is better within a clique rather than on the outside?
3 Are you looking for social status that will prove you're good enough and popular?

> "I'd do anything to be part of the popular clique. All the boys like them and all the girls want to be like them. I don't stand a chance of getting in though, because I am not pretty and I don't have much to offer."
>
> **Ella, 12**

Do you really want to be in that clique?

If you want to be in a clique you need to first question whether you share the values of this group and whether you'd be happy being a part of them? Do you want to be associated with a group who excludes other girls and tells you how you need to act and sometimes dress? Are you willing to let go of your own beliefs and be 'ruled' by someone just because they are popular?

If you want to be part of a clique because being on the outside makes you feel unwanted and unpopular, you should bear in mind that being friends with girls like these will just make your insecure feelings worse. It will also stop you making real friendships that do the things that friendships are supposed to do: make you feel good about yourself, approved of and happy.

If you don't belong to a clique, trying to get into one is a self-defeating exercise, because if you *don't* get in you'll feel as if you have failed, and if you *do* get in you'll be trapped. If you want to feel like you belong and feel valued, you are better off finding friends who share your interests and beliefs and like you for who you are, not what you represent or how you look and behave.

The way to do this is to get involved in things that interest you, whether it's sport, green issues, dance or something arty. It doesn't have to be at school, and it doesn't have to be cool (the aim is to please yourself, not others). Become part of something you enjoy and you'll see that there is a diverse world out there full of people who aren't narrow in their judgement and mean in the way they behave to others. Finding real friendships and discovering the power of how they feel will help bolster your self-esteem and how you feel about yourself, and they will keep you strong in the face of cliques who rule your school.

The sidekicks

> "I'm in a clique and sometimes it's nice to know we're looked up to and people want to be like us, but most of the times I feel like I am always being told what to do and what I should wear and say. It's hard on the inside."
>
> **Leah 13**

If you're a sidekick in a clique, ask yourself these questions:

1 Do your friendships within the clique make you feel happy?
2 Do you approve of the behaviour of the clique?
3 Are you scared of the leader of your clique?

The chances are that as a sidekick you are afraid of losing your position in the clique and becoming an outsider, so you spend much of your time pandering to what others want you to do. Research shows that because clique members are often afraid of being alienated they use strategies such as manipulation to try to preserve their status. As a result you are likely to be fairly low in self-esteem. Be aware that being in a clique won't bolster your self-esteem, even if you're in the most popular group at school. What will make you feel better, however, is keeping your friendships open and diverse, and this means breaking free of the rules that keep you in a clique and opening yourself up to new friendships.

This can be hard to do, especially if you're afraid of being bullied for breaking out. So, one good way is to start finding and maintaining friendships outside of school and in areas where your clique has no power. Volunteer or join a group, make friends with people who aren't part of a clique or who perhaps aren't even your age; it will help you to see how different you are when you're away from a controlling power.

Consider the difference in how you feel, as this will give you the courage to start stepping away from friends who aren't good for you and don't allow you to be who you want to be.

Handling mean behaviour

"The girls in my class call me fat and 'pork pie' and laugh at me during PE. I laugh it off, but I hate myself. I wish I was thin, then they'd leave me alone."
Jess, 12

"The in-girls in my class sent a group email to everyone telling them not to be my friend on Facebook. I didn't realise what was happening at first because everyone turned me down, then my best friend told me what had happened. I don't know what I did to deserve this."
Becca, 13

The old adage 'sticks and stones may break my bones, but words will never hurt me' couldn't be further from the truth. Words not only hurt but they can also stick in your head for months, or even years, after the event making you feel low about yourself and full of shame and humiliation. Which is why name-calling, being gossiped about, having your reputation ruined, being subjected to the silent treatment and being excluded (whereby girls exclude you from being friends with them, exclude you from being invited out and make you feel alone) are all forms of bullying that need to be tackled not ignored.

Name calling, catty remarks and bullying can also rip through your self-esteem faster than anything, because it's aim is to make you feel ashamed of who you are. This then leads to you wanting to hide your feelings and stay quiet about what's happening to you, which then increases your anxiety and fear, and makes you easy prey for others. It's a horrible thing to go through, but if it's happening to you staying quiet won't improve the situation. To handle being targeted:

1   Tell someone you trust – a friend, a parent, and/or a relative. Explain how the bullying is making you feel in terms of your emotions and fears, and explain exactly what's happening.

2   Take action to stop the bullying by telling a parent what's happening to you in terms of physical, verbal and mental bullying. (Alternatively, tell a teacher or call a confidential bullying line – see Resources.)

3   Come up with a plan together with the person you speak to on how to deal with what's happening. Do you want to face and talk to the bully? Do you want to ask your parents to go to the school? Do you want to talk to a teacher about what's going on and ask them to stop what's happening?

4   If the bullying has become threatening and aggressive, keep all evidence of what's been sent to you, said to you and done to you. If it's become violent, consider involving the police.

5   If the bullying takes place at vulnerable times when you're alone, such as on the way home from school or during the lunch hour, come up with solutions to ensure you're always with someone. Get someone to meet you at the school gates; eat lunch with a friend away from the crowds.

6 See a counsellor about how the bullying has affected your confidence. Talk about what you have been through, and differentiate the bullying from who you are as a person to help improve your self-esteem.

7 Remember there is no rhyme or reason to why you have been targeted. Popular people are bullied just as much as those who stick to themselves.

8 Don't pretend it's not happening, even if an incident seems small. If it's upset you and made you feel bad, it's worth talking about.

9 Address your feelings of shame. A natural response to being bullied is to feel ashamed and humiliated that it has happened to you. It's not your fault, so talk to someone about what's happening.

10 Build a strong social support system out of school. Having friends and a group you belong to away from the bullies can reboot your self-esteem and help you to see that you're a worthwhile and valuable person.

Friends who are enemies

Friends who make you feel bad, undermine your ideas, and manipulate and plot against you are friends who are enemies. The problem with friends who are enemies is that they are hard to spot, because most of the time they seem as if they are good friends and you can usually have a pretty good time with them. However, they can massively affect your self-esteem because what they do is slowly make you doubt yourself and take away your confidence by using their position as a trusted friend to attack your weak areas (the parts of you that you feel sensitive about), usually in order to make themselves feel better.

The reasons behind why friends act like this are diverse, but they include: jealousy, having a low self-esteem, and just plain mean behaviour. You have a friend who is an enemy if:

• She uses something you have told her in confidence against you.

• She tells you hurtful things for 'your benefit'.

• She says she is the only true friend you have and you should be grateful.

• You come away from being with her feeling horrible about yourself.

• She spreads gossip and lies about you but then pretends she hasn't.

• She makes you feel small and useless.

• She attacks your body shape or tries to make you feel you should diet.

• She tells you that boys don't like you.

• She gets angry when you try to make new friends.

• When you confront her behaviour she makes out you're imagining it or are paranoid.

> "My best friend Lizzie just went off with another girl. They stand laughing together, and whenever I come over, they just stop talking. I don't know what I have done."
> **Lucy, 12**
>
> "My mum is always saying, 'Is Anna your best friend, because she doesn't seem like she is?' It annoys me because I know she doesn't like Anna, because Anna is always telling me I am fat and need to lose weight and that boys don't like me, but she's just telling the truth."
> **Charlotte, 13**

What can you do?

Strategies to deal with a friend like this include being upfront about her behaviour, telling her how she has made you feel and offering her a chance to change. If that doesn't work, the only solution is to slowly expand your other friendships and move away from her. Toxic friendships, where people have agendas (issues that are about them, not you), are harmful to your self-esteem, and it's only by pulling away that you can see this.

Remember: a good friend will make you feel good about yourself; she won't try to manipulate you and you won't come away from being with her feeling horrible about yourself. If you feel those things, the chances are that your friendship is more than a little toxic and you need to either change what's happening between you or change friends.

Being an outsider

It can feel near impossible to bolster your self-esteem when you suddenly find yourself with no friends or with friends who have turned on you. Having no friends can happen for all kinds of reasons: perhaps you're the new girl, or you have fallen out with a group of girls you used to like, or you just don't seem to click with the girls at your school. Friends who have turned on you can also do so for a variety of causes, sometimes to do with jealousy, other times because of misunderstandings and yet others because your friends are bored and have nothing better to do than pick on someone.

If friends have turned on you, started spreading rumours and made hurtful comments that get to the very heart of you, be aware that you need to tell someone what's going on. It's not about getting someone to stop their mean behaviour but about being able to express how hurt and alone you feel. If you can't talk to someone you know, such as a relative, parent or older friend, try a confidential helpline (see Resources). Talking a problem through is very powerful, because it can help you to:

1 See that it's not your fault.
2 Come up with strategies to cope.
3 Work out what you want to do next.

"When I was in primary school I had lots of friends, but when I came to this school people started being mean to me. My best friend went off with someone new and spread all these catty comments about me that everyone believes. It's destroyed my confidence about myself."

Cammie, 13

What should you do?

Sometimes all you may want to do is let it blow over, but at other times you may feel that you want to take action for the sake of your feelings and your confidence. Action could be confronting your 'friend' about what she's doing and telling her to stop (although only do this if there is no physical threat from her). If you choose this method, don't be apologetic when you speak. You are not at fault, so don't give her all the power. To help yourself:

1 Be clear about what you want to say and how you're going to say it.

2 Maintain eye contact, and hold your head high when you speak to her.

3 Practise what you're going to say with your mum or a friend before approaching her.

4 Speak firmly and tell her how she has upset you and what you want her to do about it.

5 Know your outcome before you talk to her. Do you want an apology, a promise that she'll stop being mean, or just for her to leave you alone?

Coping strategies if you don't want to confront your ex-friend are to avoid her, but don't hide from her. Build up another set of friends who perhaps you didn't spend much time with before. If the problem escalates and you start to feel bullied, humiliated and picked on, this is bullying and you need to take stronger action (see Handling mean behaviour on page 89).

Feeling alone

> "I feel totally lonely. I have no friends. I feel invisible."
> **Becky, 13**

If you have no friends and/or you just don't feel you click with the girls at your school, be aware that you are not alone. Ask the adults you know and you'll find that plenty have gone through school feeling like an outsider. Sometimes because they are academically inclined (and other people look down on this), other times because they like different things to everyone else (such as music or a certain look) and other times because they had a strong friendship group outside of school.

If, however, you feel invisible and want to make friends, there are ways to let others in:

1 **Think if there is anyone who likes you**. This could be someone who's friendly towards you, or smiles in your direction or always sits by you. These are all friendship signs that you could pick up on and build a friendship from.

2 **If no one stands out, consider your interests**. What groups or activities are there at school that play to your strengths and interests? Joining a debate group, an art group or even a sport's team can all help you to meet like-minded people who could be friends.

3 **Does your reputation precede you?** Are you known as 'Aggressive Girl', 'Scary Girl' or 'Strange Girl'? If you play up to

your reputation, because it makes you angry that people don't give you a chance, consider giving people a chance first. Yes, it's stupid that people believe what they hear, but if you're a self-fulfilling prophecy, then all you are doing is putting up a barrier to others. Go out of your way to show them the real you – be friendly, smile and say something nice. It may mean moving out of your comfort zone, but it will be worth it.

4 Forget about being popular. Who wants to peak when they are 12, 13 or 14 years old? You have years ahead of you to be popular – be yourself and be happy with that.

Lastly, don't suffer in silence if you feel alone at school. Not having friends isn't something to be ashamed about or feel humiliated by. Often circumstances such as changing schools, or personality factors such as shyness, can stop you being able to connect with people. It doesn't mean you're unworthy or aren't measuring up, or that you're some kind of social misfit. Talk to someone you trust about how you feel (try a sibling or a friend outside your school) and try to come up with ways you could expand your life to meet new people. Above all, remember that life is not about how many friends you have or how many people like you back, but how much you like yourself and how much you value yourself as a person.

Being the popular girl

Are you super popular? The alpha-girl in your class with good looks, friends at your feet, boys at your beck and call – and probably the teachers too? If so, someone looking on from the outside probably thinks you don't need to read a book about feeling gorgeous inside and out, because you're the epitome of that very thing. Except, you're probably not.

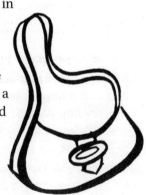

Talk to any popular girl and you'll find that below the surface of popularity

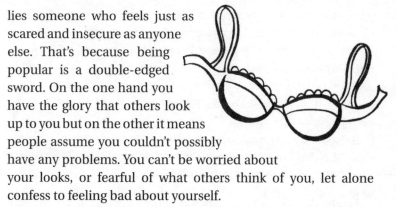

lies someone who feels just as scared and insecure as anyone else. That's because being popular is a double-edged sword. On the one hand you have the glory that others look up to you but on the other it means people assume you couldn't possibly have any problems. You can't be worried about your looks, or fearful of what others think of you, let alone confess to feeling bad about yourself.

What's more, if you dare to say any of the above, the chances are that others think you're being a drama queen. This leaves being popular a fairly lonely place to be. Here are some other things that girls have said about the perils of being popular:

> "People expect me to be perfect all the time."
> **Tara, 14**
>
> "I often feel like a fake who has to live up to other people's images."
> **Leila, 12**
>
> "I feel like I have to be what other people want me to be."
> **Jaswinder, 13**

If you're popular but feel like a fake, or you feel lonely or insecure (or all of these things and more), you need to know that popularity needn't be a trap.

Being popular isn't your job. The more you make being popular who you are, the more you will feel you have to maintain that position. Which means the more anxious you will feel about it, the more stressed you will be and the harder you will be on yourself to act perfectly.

Are you being mean ?

Being popular and being mean don't go hand in hand. If they do, you need to look at your values and your behaviour, and see if they are in sync. If they are, you need to ask yourself why you feel the need to exert power over other girls. Does it make you feel stronger? Or more in control? Or does it help squash the parts of yourself you can't face. If you feel a fake and

that no one knows you or what it's really like to be you, start talking to someone you trust. Another adult, a parent or even a helpline can help you untangle who you feel you have to be from who you are.

Lastly, forget perfection. Many popular girls feel like they have to score an A grade in every area of their life. Embrace being less than perfect – it will take a load of weight off your shoulders.

Improving your friendship skills

Good self-esteem also comes from having a sense of belonging, believing that we're capable, and knowing we are valued and worthwhile, which is why knowing how to be a good friend and how to build friendships can improve your confidence and help you feel good about yourself. Here's how to do it:

Learn to show empathy

Empathy is about identifying with another person's feelings and seeing life through her eyes not your own. For example, when your friend says she's having a hard time, it's not right to say, 'I know what you mean, I'm also having a hard time because ...' and making the conversation all about you. It's about listening, understanding what's being said, and telling your friend that you hear what she's saying.

Make time for your friends

Being able to give your friends your attention and time sends the message that you think they are important and valuable. This means taking a moment to call them back when they've called asking for your help, no matter how busy you are. Making eye contact when they are talking, so that it's clear you're listening, and making sure you remember important facts, shows you care enough to retain vital information about them.

Don't be a people pleaser

It's good to care about your friends and want to help them and be there for them, but not if you do it at the expense of your own needs. People-pleasing is also known as being a doormat, and letting friends walk all over you is a sign of low self-esteem. To improve your friendships, instigate boundaries that ensure friends don't take advantage of you. Let friends know you're willing to help but not willing to bend over backwards for them all the time.

Don't be afraid of your emotions

If you feel angry or sad that a friend has hurt you, it's OK to express that emotion, such as telling them how they have made you feel (rather than ignoring them or sulking). Being brave enough to show a range of emotions to your friends in an appropriate way is good for your friendships and good for your self-esteem, because it helps you to realise that you can be your true self to be liked.

Don't label your friends

Although we all morph to fit a situation, changing yourself into something you feel others want you to be – the fun friend, the mad friend, the clever friend – is a road to low self-esteem. Just as you shouldn't dictate to friends who they are, don't let them label you, even if that label is flattering and nice. Labels trap us into a certain role and make it hard for us to become an all-round person, which is what having a healthy self-esteem is all about.

Don't gossip too much

When it comes to limiting gossiping, it's easier said than done, I know. Everyone gossips, because most of us love to talk about our friends (in good and bad ways) and get a thrill from hearing juicy news. The problem is that gossip is often hurtful. It can ruin someone's reputation, and be used by other girls to improve their standing by destroying someone else's. If you don't think you gossip, consider how much of your daily conversation revolves around talking about your friends and speculating on what they've done and why.

Dealing with parents

Parents are a very tricky subject: on the one hand we love them and don't want to let them down, but on the other they nag at us, and can make us feel bad about ourselves – often without realising it. Which is why, if you want to improve your self-esteem, it's important to know how to deal with your parents and their issues.

Quiz: Who's bringing you down?

For the following questions tick the answer that seems closest for you, then add your scores up at the end to see who is bringing you down.

1 **When you look in the mirror, who's negative voice do you hear telling you you're overweight/unattractive?**
   a. Your mum
   b. Your dad
   c. Yourself

2 Who makes you feel the most horrible about yourself?

 a. Your mum

 b. Yourself

 c. Your dad

3 Who do you feel least understands you?

 a. Your mum

 b. You

 c. Your dad

4 When your parents try to talk to you, are you:

 a. Open to what they say

 b. Defensive

 c. Immediately angry

5 When you're in a bad mood, who are you most likely to take it out on?

 a. Your mum

 b. Yourself

 c. Your dad

Scores

1.	a	10	b	5	c 0
2.	a	10	b	0	c 5
3.	a	10	b	0	c 5
4.	a	5	b	10	c 0
5.	a	10	b	0	c 5

0–5 Parental problem
You probably don't need me to tell you this but your relationship with your parents needs work. See below for help

5–20 Dad problem
Your relationship with your dad is faltering and maybe even making your life a misery. See below for help.

40–50 Mum problem
Are you constantly fighting with your mum? See below for help.

Some of us are blessed with parents who encourage us, let us be who we are, and comfort us when we feel down and sad. Others, however, are not so lucky, and have parents who break their confidence (often without realising it) and leave them feeling rotten and bad about themselves. However you feel about your parents, what's important to know is that they are human. This means that they make mistakes, just like you and I, they aren't always right and they make a mess of stuff, even when they have your best interests at heart. That's not giving them a get-out clause, but it's hopefully helping you to see that they aren't perfect, especially when it comes to knowing how to make you feel good about yourself.

> "My parents are always telling me in subtle ways that I am not good enough. They say I need to lose weight for my health, make more of myself for my own good and try harder at school, unless I want to be a loser! So, basically, what they are saying is they think I am fat, ugly and stupid."
>
> **Jada, 14**

When it comes to self-esteem, parents can get it alarmingly wrong. They can make you feel small, not good enough, stupid and ugly, and all without realising it, just by the way they speak to you and their throwaway comments (quick remarks or ideas that are not intended to be hurtful, but probably weren't thought about carefully). Which is why it's important to tackle your issues with how they talk to you, otherwise the issues will just follow you into adult-hood. Below are just some of the ways your parents may be inadvertently lowering your esteem and how you can tackle them.

Mothers and daughters

Many mothers have a hard time when they see their daughters growing up and pulling away from them. Although it's natural and normal to want to identify more with your friends than your mum when you're a teenager, your mum will be trying to do the opposite and do everything she can to make herself feel closer to you (a direct result of knowing you're pulling away). This is one of the main reasons why mums often insist she and you are alike and one of the main reasons why girls feel their mums don't know them.

'You're just like me.'

> "My mother is always telling people we're like twins. We're not. She's 35 and I am 13. I don't like what she likes, I don't dress like her and I am not her in any way at all."
>
> **Lily, 13**

What you have to do: realise this is about your mum feeling worried that she is losing you, not about her wanting you to be a mini version of her.

You don't have to be her, for her to approve and love you (ask her if you don't believe me). What can make this situation better and improve your sense of self, is to try to build a grown-up relationship with her, where you talk about what's worrying you and making you feel bad.

To do this, try to maintain everyday communication with her. Talk to her about the small stuff, keep the lines of communication open and this will show her that although you're growing up, you're not necessarily growing away.

'You're always angry, just like your father.'

"My dad left my mum when I was five, and whenever I do something to make her mad she yells at me, telling me I am just like him. He was violent and nasty and I hate it that a part of him is in me."

Mel, 12

Feeling you are being identified with a negative member of your family is a great way to have your self-esteem stamped on, so what you have to do is work out if negative statements being made about you are true or not. Are you, for example, really aggressive and angry like X in your family? To find out, ask the people who know you: your friends. They will be able to tell you if this is totally wrong or something you need to work on.

Bear in mind that if it's something you need to work on, it doesn't mean you're a copy of someone else, or that you're destined to end up like them. It's more that you've become a self-fulfilling prophecy – in other words, you've been told you're bad tempered so many times that you become bad tempered. Our minds believe what we're constantly told, so tell yourself something new and positive, and keep telling yourself.

If it's not true, point this out to your mum (or whoever is saying it). Tell her that you don't feel it's true and how much it hurts when she says it.

So-called negative emotions, such as anger and sensitivity, are normal emotions that you should be allowed to express (in the appropriate way and in the right instance).

However, parents often try to suppress you (by telling you you're too angry or too uncontrollable), either because your emotion is being expressed in an out-of-proportion way to an event – such as, your brother turns the TV over and you go ballistic – or because it's an emotion they themselves have been taught to suppress.

'I hate my body, I hate your body.'

Self-esteem fact: 57 per cent of girls have a mother who criticises her own looks. (Dove, Real Girls, Real Pressure Report 2008)

The chances are that if your mother is not happy with the way she looks or her weight, you'll be a copy of her. This is because up until this point she has been the most powerful role model in your life, and so most of your behaviour you will have learned from her. So, if your mum has unhealthy attitudes towards her body image and is always telling herself she is fat and ugly, then you're likely to mimic that behaviour and feel bad about yourself.

What you have to do: tell your mum what you're hearing from her. The chances are she isn't aware of how she talks to herself about her body and yours.

Tell her how you feel when you hear her say these things. Talk about self-acceptance together and how you can both work towards feeling better about your bodies.

'Don't try that, you'll only be disappointed when you fail.'

Sometimes when your mum is on your case and seemingly putting you down, what she is really doing is being overprotective and trying to stop you from getting rejected. Unfortunately, what it feels like is a stream of negative criticism that leaves you feeling not good enough and totally discouraged.

What you have to do: talk to your mum about her views and explain how it's making you feel inside. As much as she may want to guide you, she has to remember that it's your life and that you need to be able to explore the avenues you want, fall down a few times and get back up again, in order to build belief in yourself.

Tell her what you find encouraging and what you find discouraging. Talk to her about her own feelings about ambition, academics and non-academic pursuits.

"I would love to be an actress, but my mum's always saying I'm not good enough and that I shouldn't waste time on it. When I do school plays she's really critical and says mean things. It makes me hate her."

Maya, 13

Fathers and daughters

To be shouted at, insulted and picked on is demoralising, no matter how good your self-esteem is, and it's worse when the person doing it is your father. No one deserves to be treated this way, so what you need to do is recognise that this is a parent issue. This means that your dad is at fault here and is probably doing it because of his own issues. Plus it's important to realise that parents parent you the way they were parented. Meaning, if they insult you and make you feel ashamed, the chances are that's what happened to them (though that's not an excuse but a reason why they are doing it). Plus they may not recognise the effect it has had on them, but you can recognise what it's doing to you and tell them how it makes you feel.

'You are a waste of space.'

> "My dad calls me an idiot."
> **Lou, 12**

What you have to do: if it's impossible to talk to your father and tell him how these comments are making you feel, tell another adult you trust, in confidence. Sometimes, just hearing that they are wrong can help you to keep your self-esteem high.

Tell your father how his words hurt. If this is impossible, ask your mum or a relative to step in. If nothing works, bear in mind that your dad's view is just that: his view. It's not true just because he says it.

'You can't go out dressed like that.'

> "My dad and I fight all the time about what I wear. He says my skirts are too short, I dress like a slapper, and I have no respect for myself. I hate him!"
> **Leanne, 14**

Dads have a hard time with teenage daughters, partly because they have never been a teenage girl and so don't understand the pressures that come with it, and partly because they have been a teenage boy and so understand how boys think about girls. This makes them crazy, and sometimes they act crazy. So, if you have a dad who's constantly on your case about your clothes, it's really about him wanting to protect you.

What you have to do: tell him to stop the name-calling. Tell him how it feels when he labels you something nasty or tells you that you have no taste in clothes. Consider whether your clothes are appropriate – are they OTT and designed to wind him up, or is he being OTT about what you're wearing? It can help to have another point of view here, like your mum or another person he listens to.

Find a middle ground where you can compromise over clothes. Perhaps dress down for school but wear what you want when you're with friends. Ask him what his real issue with your clothes is? Does he really think you're being a 'slapper' (or whatever he calls you) or is he afraid that this is how others will judge you when they see what you're wearing?

'You were such a nice little girl.'

"My dad refuses to see me as a grown up. He calls me his little girl all the time and gets angry if I talk about boys or accuses me of being not so nice any more."
Emma 12

Dads have a harder time than mums do at seeing their daughters as teenagers on the brink of adulthood. For many dads this is about not being able to see their daughters as women with their own minds and thoughts, and is often worse if you grew up being 'daddy's little girl'. For many dads it's a control issue and a fear one: they are worried that if they don't try to control you, you'll grow away from them.

What you have to do: maintain communication with your dad. Tell him what his comments make you feel about yourself. Find ways to have common interests that still bind you together, such as watching a TV programme together or listening to music.

Talk to your mum about how you feel, and come up with ways to help your father see that you are growing up.

Refuse to let his analysis of you affect your self-esteem. You probably *were* a nice little girl, but that doesn't mean you're not

Ten ways to handle your parents

1 Tell them how their hurtful comments make you feel about yourself.

2 Don't be on the defensive when you talk to them; listen before you react.

3 If they won't believe in you, believe in yourself – this is where success begins.

4 Be what you want to be, not what they want you to be. They are your parents, but it's not your job to fulfil their dreams.

5 Ask your parents how their parents treated them. It can help to remind them how they felt as teenagers, and it can help you to see where they are coming from.

6 Don't make assumptions about your parents and what they expect from you – ask them.

7 Consider if criticism is constructive before you throw it back at them.

8 If they don't get you, take the time to tell them, or show them, who you are.

9 Try to stay calm when talking. Shouting and getting angry, especially when you're upset, leads to an escalation in emotions and will trigger the same reaction in your parents.

10 Some parents are just not open to criticism no matter how constructive. If your parents refuse to listen to you, shout you down or tell you you're not feeling what you're feeling, it pays to talk to someone else. Try a friend's mum, a teacher you trust or a relative. It may not help you to manage your parents any better, but it will help to make you feel better.

wonderful now that you're older and have your own thoughts and views.

'Girls are so …'

> "My dad is so sexist he's always commenting on how fat some women are (he's fat but he doesn't talk about that) or saying how great a woman's legs or breasts are. It makes me feel sick to hear him and makes me wonder what he thinks about me."
>
> **Jade 15**

Having a father who speaks disrespectfully about women, or believes women should behave in a certain way, or even views women as objects, can have a detrimental effect on how you feel about your body and your future relationship with boys.

What you have to do: ask your mum to talk to him, explaining how his views make you feel about yourself. Challenge what he's saying by telling him it hurts or offends you. Give him a chance; he may not be aware of how his behaviour is affecting you. Some habits die hard.

Dealing with boys

Whether you have a boyfriend, want a boyfriend or are wondering what it's like to have a boyfriend, it's worth knowing the effect boys, love and relationships can have on your self-esteem. The fact is that when it comes to relationships and boys we all feel at our most vulnerable. Who hasn't felt left out when all their friends get asked out and they don't? Or felt the misery of rejection when someone you fancy asks your best friend out or ignores you when you say hello?

The problem with venturing into relationships, however, is that having low self-esteem not only makes a bad relationship worse, or causes a potentially good one to break, but it can also help make you feel as if you're never going to find love or have a boy ask you out.

> "I am always the girl boys are friends with. I take the messages to the pretty girls and then have to pretend I am fine when they get asked out."
>
> **Rosie, 14**

Quiz: Your views on love

For the following questions draw a circle around the answer that seems closest for you, then add up your scores at the end.

1 Do you feel that having a boyfriend is the answer to your problems?

Yes

No

2 Do you feel that it's only pretty girls who get asked out?

Yes

No

3 Do you feel there is something wrong with you because no boy fancies you?

Yes

No

4 When you fancy a boy do you take on his interests such as football, and/or the bands he likes?

Yes

No

5 To keep a boyfriend should you work hard to be what he wants?

Yes

No

6 Are you attracted to boys who don't treat you well?

Yes

No

7 Are you secretly worried you're going to be single forever?

Yes

No

8 Do you believe in the 'treat them mean; keep them keen' theory?

Yes

No

Scores

More than 6 yeses
Your self-esteem levels are definitely affecting your views on love and relationships. You need to bolster who you are before throwing yourself into love, or you could end up in bad relationships that bring you down.

More than 3 yeses
You are putting too much emphasis on love and relationships, whether it's by giving boys all the power or by assuming you are nothing without a date. What's important is not who wants to go out with you but why you want to go out with them.

Fewer than 2 yeses
You have a healthy view of yourself and so a healthy view of love and relationships, but be wary of how easy it is to let love and boys bring you down.

The truth about boys is that they can also have low self-esteem, body image problems, anxieties about falling in love and fears about who they are, which, in a nutshell, means boyfriends aren't the answer to your problems. Getting one may momentarily make you feel wanted and approved of, but having a relationship for the wrong reasons is the kiss of death to your self-esteem. Here's why:

A boyfriend won't make you feel more attractive

You may feel as if you have been 'chosen' and therefore must have some good points, but in the long term being with someone won't improve how you feel about yourself. In fact it may ruin your relationship if all you're in it for is to feel good about yourself. What's more, being with someone just for the sake of it can make you terrified of being left, and so it may make you do things like squashing your true self or getting involved in stuff you're not ready for, just to keep someone happy.

A boyfriend won't make you feel more lovable

If you don't love who you are and also believe you have lovable qualities, no person will ever be able to make you feel loved. What's more, part of you will always wonder what the heck he sees in you, and so you'll either be eager for constant reassurance (exhausting for your boyfriend) or be someone who 'tests' what he is saying to you through silly games like jealousy and possessiveness.

Sorting out the love myths from reality

Love fact: new research suggests that teens who regularly watch romance-based dramas are more likely to have traditional views about dating (such as boys should ask the girls out) and believe women shouldn't be strong and independent.

When it comes to boys, relationships and your self-esteem, it's important to understand reality from myth so that you don't fall prey to what others want you to believe and do.

Reality check 1: liking someone doesn't mean they'll like you back

This is a sad fact of relationships. Just because you really, really like someone and know in your heart that you'd be perfect together, and maybe even get on like a house on fire, if he doesn't like you back, he simply doesn't like you back. This means that nothing you do or say will get him to change his mind. So don't feel that you are not measuring up as you are and that you have to be something you're not to win him over. The chances are his decision has nothing to do with you, perhaps he isn't ready for a relationship (remember boys mature a lot later than girls) or perhaps he likes someone else. Making it all about you will just stamp on your self-esteem.

Reality check 2: being single doesn't mean no one fancies you

Being single just means you haven't yet met someone you want to date – and that's all it means. It doesn't mean you're a loser or a person lacking in the stuff boys want. Take it personally and all you'll be doing is making yourself feel desperate for no reason. There is more to life than boys and dating, just ask your mum, or remember back a few years when this was the last thing on your mind.

Reality check 3: being dumped/ rejected doesn't mean you did something wrong

See reality check 1 above. It may feel like you did something wrong but the reality is that being dumped and rejected rarely have anything to with your personality or behaviour (and when it does, boys usually say so). Mostly it has to do with circumstances such as teen relationships being a testing ground where people discover what they want and what they like, which is why relationships start and are over at lightning speed.

Reality check 4: someone who treats you badly or abusively doesn't love you

It's a hard but painful truth, but someone who treats you badly (cheats, talks to you disrespectfully, stands you up or lets you down) and someone who is physically or mentally abusive to you, doesn't love you, no matter what they say. They may try to tell you it's your fault they are abusing you or apologise and promise it will never happen again but the reality is you need to break free of this relationship – and fast.

Myth 1: everyone's having sex

Everyone may say they are having sex, but endless studies show they are not. And even if everyone is, so what? Sex is not a race, and it's not a competition, and it's really nobody's business but yours – so don't be lulled into thinking sex is something you should be considering, or trying out.

Myth 2: boys who like you play hard to get

Boys who like you don't play hard to get, they tend to flirt, show you they like you and make a play for you.

Myth 3: boys like girls who are busty/thin/quiet

This is a myth that girls spread about and boys play up to. If you're not being asked out, it can be easy to tell yourself it's because you're not X, Y or Z. The reality is that you can only be who you are, nothing more and nothing less. Try to be what you think boys want you to be and you risk losing yourself completely.

Myth 4: all's fair in love and war

This is a load of nonsense and something people say to justify mean behaviour, gossiping, name calling and cheating in the name of love. If you want a boy to like you for yourself and feel loved for who you are, you need to show him who you are, stay within what you believe is right and wrong and treat him well.

Dealing with you

We all feel under pressure. Apart from the anxieties about what you look like and who you're friends with, there is the pressure about who you are and how you feel you're measuring up in the world. You may not think you put yourself under any pressure, but the chances are you're doing it.

Whereas some of this is natural and normal, it's important to see what the expectations are that you have for yourself and work out if you're making yourself feel better or worse.

Quiz: How hard are you on yourself?

For the following questions tick the answer that seems closest for you, then add up all your answers that were followed by the letter (P), then (OA) and then (OS):

1 You're having a party, but just as people start to arrive you spill juice over your clothes. How do you feel:
   a. You put on a brave face but feel your party is now completely ruined. (P)
   b. Ignore it and race around making sure everyone's having a good time, and the music is good and there is plenty of food. (OA)
   c. Embarrassed and humiliated. (OS)

2 You think people like you because:
   a. You make sure there is nothing not to like. (P)
   b. You're good fun, nice and clever and a good friend. (OA)
   c. You're not sure people do like you. (OS)

3 **When you fall out with a friend, you:**

    a. Feel worried about what you've done wrong. (P)

    b. Feel worried about what you haven't done. (OA)

    c. Feel worried that they have always hated you. (OS)

4 **The real you is:**

    a. Always worried you're not getting something right. (P)

    b. Always worried you're not good enough. (OA)

    c. Always worried people are judging you. (OS)

5 **You'd be happy if:**

    a. You could get things right all the time. (P)

    b. You had more time to do the things you wanted to do. (OA)

    c. You didn't see slights everywhere. (OS)

Scores

Mostly Ps

You're a perfectionist; see below for advice on this.

Mostly OAs

You're an over-achiever; see below for advice on this.

Mostly OSs

You're oversensitive; see below for advice on this.

Perfectionist

Perfectionism stems from a belief that you aren't good enough just being you and so you have to excel in order to be loved or liked. Having high standards is a good thing, but making yourself feel terrible because you never reach them or if you make a mistake, or avoiding things because you might not be perfect is not so good.

The other problem with perfectionism is that it increases anxiety and can lead to feelings of panic and panic attacks. This means it's essential to get this under control before it influences more than your self-esteem.

> "I am a total perfectionist. I can't bear it if I don't look right, or if I don't make high marks. I drive myself mad sometimes trying to make stuff perfect, but it makes me feel good."
> **Lily, 13**

What you have to realise: it's OK to make mistakes. We all make them; they are a part of life.

1 Make yourself do something where you don't excel, and take pride in the fact that you are taking a risk and doing something different.

2 Don't idolise others. They may look perfect but all you're doing is not seeing them as a real person.

3 Feel good about your accomplishments, even if they are not perfect. If you don't feel good about yourself now, will you ever?

4 Let people see that you're willing to be not quite perfect. It's uncomfortable at first, but it will help others to see you as a real person, not a perfection machine.

5 Finally, remember: you can be smart without having to be the smartest. You can have friends without having to be the most popular and you can be sporty without having to be the best.

Over-achiever

Over-achieving is another way you might try to make up for not feeling good enough. Over-achievers stay in constant motion, racking up friends, interests, good grades and more, as a way of trying to feel loved and accepted, but inside they feel the opposite. Like perfectionism, over-achieving comes from a belief (usually created in childhood) that it's doing things that gets you love and approval, so the more you do the more you'll be liked and accepted. This is the opposite of having a healthy self-esteem where you feel good about yourself even if you haven't achieved something or been given approval.

"It's like I feel I have to be the most fun person, the cleverest in my class, the person with the most friends, someone who's good at sport. It's exhausting."
Dani, 13

If you're an over-achiever: consider how you can expect to feel good enough if you keep moving the goalposts of what it means to measure up.

1 Ask the people you love and like what it is they love and like about you. You'll be surprised that it has less to do with about what you have achieved and more about who you are as a person.

2 Instead of being focused on pleasing parents and teachers, think about what would make you happy and feel better (try brainstorming this with friends).

3 Rather than seeking approval for your achievements, practise feeling good about what you've achieved, and use it to have confidence in your abilities.

4 Talk to someone about how you feel inside with regard to your anxiety, depression and your fears. Over-achieving usually covers up issues that you need to express.

Over-sensitive

Being sensitive to others is one thing, but being over-sensitive, whereby everything people say and do hurts you in some way is a self-esteem killer. You know you're over-sensitive if a bad-hair day becomes a disaster when your mum comments on it, or a friend choosing to have lunch with someone else reduces you to abject misery. At the core of being over-sensitive is constantly worrying. Worrying that you don't look good enough, worrying that you say the right things or that others accept you as being good enough.

> "I am always being told I am over-sensitive, but I can't help it. I take offence at everything, get hurt when people tease me and find myself replaying situations in my head where someone has hurt me."
>
> **Beth, 13**

To help yourself: you need to change your way of thinking.

1 Remind yourself that you won't feel bad or hurt unless you think of the situation as a hurtful one or a bad one. For example, a friend chooses to sit with someone else. Is she purposely avoiding you or is she just eating her lunch? Ask her what's happened without accusing her or making your hurt feelings her problem.

2 Worrying is linked to helplessness. We worry when we feel helpless because it makes us feel that we're dealing with a situation that we have no control over. In reality, worrying just increases anxiety and doesn't help in any way. Think of a more productive way to deal with a worry, such as talking it through with someone.

3 Work out when someone is being insensitive – making a personal comment that is aimed to hurt you or – if someone's making a throwaway comment. A clue is their reaction to your reaction. If they looked shocked or surprised that you're upset, it was a throwaway comment.

4 Take the spotlight off yourself by realising that everyone is too busy worrying about themselves to notice how you look or what you say all the time.

Lastly, bear in mind that feeling anxious, unwanted, fearful about life and misunderstood are all teenage rites of passage.

Just as feeling happy and secure comes and goes, so too will these emotions. What you have to do is learn to keep everything you feel in perspective so that they don't start to define who you are and make you feel less of a person.

The way to do this is to accept both the good parts and bad parts of yourself, as well as the sensitive and not so sensitive parts! It's not an easy thing to do, but it's something even the most well adjusted person you know has had to come to terms with. Some of this is about learning from your mistakes, but a big part of it is about forgiving yourself for making mistakes (and/or for being mean or nasty). We can all be bad, but that doesn't mean we're horrible people who don't deserve to be happy. What matters is not what you've done or how you've behaved but what you have learned from your behaviour and what you choose to do next.

Chapter Four

Gorgeous for Life

Being gorgeous for life is about having the right attitude. One that accepts you're less than perfect, nice as well as nasty and good as well as bad. As we've seen in Chapter Two, it's about accepting that your body has flaws, but celebrating the fact that you are healthy and strong, and full of your own kind of beauty. It's also about not being too hard on yourself, as we've seen in Chapter Three, not hating who you are and, above all, not letting others stamp all over your self-esteem. It's a tall order, but one that's not so hard to get right if you give yourself a break and accept that sometimes you'll get it wrong, and sometimes you'll get it right.

Alongside all of the above – which is primarily about work on the inside – is getting to grips with how you feel about the outside of yourself. Although much of this has to do with bolstering your body image and loving yourself warts and all, it's also about treating your body well, because the lower your self-esteem, the less you're likely to take care of yourself and the less likely you are to make the most of who you are. Which is why this part is about the surface stuff, such as how to look good and to get to grips with beauty issues, as well as

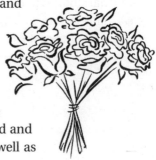

finding a style that brings out the best in you. Sometimes, when you're feeling rough, transforming the outside really will make you feel better.

Looking after your body

To exude body confidence it's important to think in terms of being 'healthy' and 'in shape' rather than fat or thin, because it's health that counts, not just in terms of your physical health but also your mental health. If you can focus on being healthy, you're going to feel fit, strong and able as opposed to always feeling not right. This means not just focusing on the food you eat (or don't eat) but also on your activity levels and the bad habits you may have picked up. Here's how to do it.

> "I eat once a day, because I want to lose weight. It makes me feel tired, irritable and has me dying to eat all day."
> **Louise, 14**

The basics of healthy eating

When it comes to food, there's a lot written about what's healthy and what's not. Whereas some of it is obvious – food loaded in sugar and fat are unhealthy, whereas fruit and vegetables are healthy – some of it isn't so obvious. Which is why this section's all about the basics of healthy eating. It's not so that you can lose loads of weight and/or start controlling what you eat but that you can understand how what you choose to eat will affect how you feel. What's more, it's important to be aware of the fundamentals of healthy eating, because the eating habits you form now tend to become the ones you follow as an adult. Those are the ones you then have trouble breaking later in life when you have to for the sake of your health.

What is food?

Food is basically our body's fuel, which means what you put in to your body affects what you get out of it. Too much fat, and sugar (yes, we're talking fast food, crisps and sweets) and you're going to crash and burn, then leave yourself feeling depressed, lethargic and, frankly, ready for bed by 3.00 pm (more on this later). Having said that, unhealthy food is something we all indulge in, with one survey finding that the favourite food for teens is burgers followed by chocolate, pizza, fried chicken and a fizzy cola. The survey also found that one in 12 teenagers were eating these things more than seven times a week and more than once a day.

The good news is that you don't have to avoid junk food and fast food totally. If you eat it in moderation – that is, alongside the healthy stuff and less than seven times a week – you'll be fine. Any more than this and you need to be aware of the following:

1 **Too much fat in your food** equals weight gain and lethargy. High-fat foods are crisps, pizza, burgers and chips.

Fast foods such as hamburgers, pizza, and fried chicken and chips, contain large amounts of saturated fat. This not only causes you to put on weight but is also a risk factor in heart disease. Too much saturated fat in your diet will make you feel lethargic because fats in food are the most concentrated source of energy. So, if you're eating too much and not burning it off through exercise, your body will store it, creating weight gain and sleepiness.

2 **Too much sugar in your food** equals irritability and bad skin. Sugary foods are biscuits, cakes, chocolate and sweets.

Sugar (alongside fat) is what makes fast foods taste so good and why it also makes it so hard to give these foods up! But the reality is that eating too much sugar will make you feel irritable, tired and cranky, because it gives you what's known as a false high. This is where you find yourself with a burst of energy only to come crashing down really quickly. Too much sugar can also be the hidden cause of a bad complexion or generally unhealthy skin, because when your body can't expel excess amounts of sugar, these sugars can trigger the growth of bacteria that can attack skin.

3 **Too much caffeine** in your drinks leads to anxiety, stress and insomnia. Caffeine drinks are fizzy colas, fizzy energy drinks, coffee and tea.

If you're a fizzy-drink addict who drinks at least three cans a day, be aware that your drink is affecting your moods. This is because drinks loaded with caffeine trigger anxiety, dizziness, headaches and probably the jitters. Caffeine can also interfere with normal sleep patterns and leave you finding it hard to fall asleep or waking up halfway through the night.

The healthy-eating rules

Eat healthily and you will:

1 Have boundless energy.

2 Feel good about your body.

3 Get all the nutrients your growing body needs.

4 Be less likely to have unhealthy eating habits.

5 Be at a weight you're happy with.

6 Sleep well.

7 Look healthy.

8 Be mentally alert.

9 Feel positive.

Food fact: studies show that teenage diets typically lack several essential nutrients. Nutrient-rich foods often come up short as meals often lack enough fruits, vegetables and milk or milk products in favour of high sugar and fat products.

(*Nationwide Food Consumption Survey*, International Food Information Council)

Simple healthy eating

When it comes to healthy eating, the trick is to:

1 **Eat foods from all the main food groups**: vegetables, fruits, fat (dairy), protein (lean meat and fish, or vegetarian alternatives, such as tofu, beans and nuts), and carbohydrates (bread, potatoes, pasta, rice).

2 **Aim for three meals a day** and a couple of snacks.

3 **Keep your portions** at the right level – so don't go super-size and monster-size on everything you eat and don't eat such small amounts that you always feel starving. The key is to limit the unhealthy stuff to, say, a small chocolate bar instead of three large ones, or simly eat three proper meals a day that incorprate point 1, above. Then stop eating when you're full, and you'll be a healthy-eating kind of girl.

4 **Don't skip meals**, especially breakfast. It's hard to get your head around this, but three meals a day with two snacks is the best way to keep your weight healthy, stop the urge to binge eat on junk food and feel good energy-wise. Skipping meals only leads to feeling hungry and overeating during the day.

5 **Don't divide foods into good and bad**. All foods can be part of healthy eating, when eaten in moderation. This means you do not need to buy low-calorie, low-carb, fat-free, or diet foods.

6 **Rate your hunger before you eat**. Before you pop something into your mouth, ask yourself if you're hungry or not. Using a score of 1 to 10, thinking of 10 as starving and 1 as being not hungry: now try to reach 5 before you eat.

7 Understand why you eat. We reach for foods (or not) for all kinds of reasons. Try to find your reasons by keeping a food diary and noting how you feel every time you eat. This can help you to understand what's behind any kind of emotional eating.

8 Don't make food the enemy. Don't let your eating habits make you feel guilty and bad or upset. Food is just food and should not control your life or have the power to make you feel 'bad'. If it does, consider talking to someone you trust about your issues around food before they escalate (see Resources).

Exercise and self-esteem

Are you the girl who skips PE every week, the person who gets the bus just to go two stops and/or begs her mum to drive her round the corner so that she doesn't have to walk? If so, you're not alone. According to the figures, although more than seven out of ten under 16s are concerned about their appearance and want to weigh less, 50 per cent of girls don't exercise even once a week (with the exception of the odd walk).

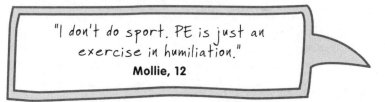

"I don't do sport. PE is just an exercise in humiliation."
Mollie, 12

Contrary to popular belief, you don't have to be good at sports or team games or even like PE to like and maybe even love exercise. The problem is PE can put girls off exercise for life because the focus is on competition and being good at sport, rather than being healthy and active. Bear in mind that even if you loathe PE, there are plenty of ways to stay active that aren't about athletics and team sports (see below for more on this). Get fit and stay active on a daily basis and you will:

• Have higher self-esteem levels than girls who don't exercise.

• Have lower stress levels and lower anxiety levels.

- Feel happy about your weight.
- Have a more positive body image.
- Feel strong and more able than girls who don't exercise.
- See your body in a more positive light.

Part of the reason why active girls feel this way is that exercise gives you what's known as an endorphin rush. These are chemicals that naturally relieve pain and lift your mood, and they are released when you exercise at a rate that gets your heart pumping. Taking part in regular exercise also makes your body physically stronger, which in turn can make you feel emotionally stronger and more appreciative of your body. Lastly, challenging yourself to do something that slightly scares you – like a new sport – and/or being good at a sport boosts your self-esteem by helping you to see that you're braver than you thought and also more talented.

It's recommended that all under-18s should get a minimum of 60 minutes of moderate-to-vigorous exercise every day of the week, with 90 minutes preferred. This doesn't mean spending days down the gym or hours running around the block. This refers to *activity*, as in the amount of time you're moving around at a moderate pace, as opposed to sitting or lying down and not doing anything.

If you're resistant to exercising, think about what may be holding you back. Common fears are:

- Feeling embarrassed about how you look when you're doing exercise.
- Feeling you're not fit enough to exercise.
- Feeling your friends/teachers would make fun of you.
- Feeling other peers would be mean if you tried.
- Not knowing where to start.
- Feeling that you're rubbish at sport, so why bother?
- Worried about a past bad experience, that has turned you off.
- Worried about how you look in sports gear.
- You have no time.

Getting over that exercise block

To change your attitude, first be aware that you don't have to be good at sport to participate in it or do it (even if peers or sports teachers make you feel this way). Exercise and sport, like any skill, improves the more you practise it and the more you do it.

Next, try talking about what's bothering you with your mother or close friends. Are there solutions to your anxieties, such as exercising at home (workout DVDs are good), or at a class some- where, or even buying yourself more comfortable workout gear?

Feeling not fit enough to exercise, or worried that you don't have time, can also be solved. Firstly you don't have to be fit to workout. The idea is that working out makes you fit, and the reality is that no one is watching. Take a look at runners out in the street – does anyone pay attention to what they're doing?

As for time issues, firstly, if you have time to watch TV (and teens watch 16–21 hours a week – that's 3 hours a day) you have time to exercise. What's more, 60–90 minutes of exercise a day doesn't have to be done all at once. You can break it up into 30 minutes before school, 30 minutes at school and another 30 after school.

Secondly, don't make it complicated; exercise that you'll keep up and enjoy should be simple and fun, and preferably in line with something you enjoy, such as music or being outside or competing. Think of the following:

- Street-dance classes
- Ballet classes
- Skating
- Running or walking
- Cycling
- Swimming
- Martial arts
- Aerobics
- Tennis
- Belly dancing

A word about compulsive exercise

Exercising compulsively, where you feel you have to exercise to control your weight or to try to achieve an unrealistic body image, is not healthy or good for you. If you put exercise ahead of friends or homework, and/or rush upstairs or out to exercise every time you eat, or if you feel anxious if you can't exercise, or fearful that you will gain weight, you need to seek help from a parent or a counsellor.

Getting rid of your bad habits

Did you know that the lower your self-esteem the more likely you are to indulge in bad habits such as binge drinking and smoking, and even self-harm? If this rings a bell in your life or in someone you know, here's how to cope.

Smoking and your self-esteem

Studies show that girls who smoke are twice as likely to be worried about their body image than non-smokers and twice as likely to indulge in extreme weight-loss strategies. This is why it's worth knowing that women who smoke weigh only a 450g (1lb) less than those who don't. What's more, smoking doesn't stop you from eating; even if you smoke to avoid certain meals, you're just likely to eat more later in the day.

Peer pressure is another factor in smoking, as is thinking that the habit gives you glamour or an edge over other girls. Although we all know that smoking kills, and that's why you should quit, did you also know that smoking kills you in the beauty stakes as well? It not only ages you, but it gives you bad breath and yellow teeth, adds wrinkles to your face by your twenties, and makes your periods more painful. Here's why:

• **Your skin**: to stay healthy, your skin relies on your body's blood supply to pump away healthily beneath the skin. Nicotine in cigarettes impedes blood flow and causes dehydration, which leads to premature wrinkles.

- **Your breath**: smoking dries out your mouth, which means deadly halitosis. So, you will have bad breath even if you chew gum or suck extra-strong mints.

- **Your teeth**: look at the teeth of any smoker and you'll see a less than Hollywood smile. Smoking also gives you gum disease and helps you to lose your teeth.

- **Your period**: according to research, women who smoke experience more severe premenstrual symptoms and have a 50 per cent increase in cramps lasting two or more days.

Reasons to quit smoking

⋆ You'll have more money.

⋆ You'll have more energy.

⋆ Your hair and clothes will smell better.

⋆ You'll look better (clearer skin for a start, especially around your lips, nose and cheeks where smoke leaves a residue).

⋆ You'll have sweeter breath, so more people will want to kiss you.

⋆ You'll have healthy-looking nails.

⋆ You'll be less jumpy.

⋆ You'll feel healthier and better about yourself.

Alcohol and your self-esteem

Do you drink to feel more confident, or because your friends drink, or because you think it makes you more grown up? Well, figures show that Britain is among the worst in Europe for teen drunkenness and alcohol abuse, with more than a quarter of 15- and 16-year-olds getting drunk at least three times a month.

That's a lot of alcohol and it's usually taken in binge amounts (when you drink a lot in a short space of time) that then directly affects your behaviour and judgement and leads you to do things you wouldn't usually do.

This is because alcohol is a drug that gives you an artificial high followed by a low that feels like depression. It's a pretty nasty combination, so if you drink, you need to consider why you feel you have to? Is it because:

- Drinking alcohol makes you feel braver?
- Your friends are all doing it?
- You like the feeling and that alcohol brings you out of yourself?
- It makes you feel more in control?

If the above statements ring true, it's worth knowing that alcohol doesn't bring out the real you, it brings out the you that doesn't have reasoning skills and inhibitions that help to protect you from danger. This then leaves you prey to a variety of risks. Statistics show that if you're drunk you're more likely to be involved in an accident, more likely to have a one-night stand you regret, more likely to succumb to peer pressure and more likely to be involved in a violent incident.

To help yourself:

1 Avoid drinking if you're under 15 (this is the recommendation by the Chief Medical Officer) as it's considered to be a danger to your health. Alcohol may be legal but it is a drug and can affect your body like poison. The smaller and younger you are, the greater its effects.

2 If you are going to drink, drink sensibly (i.e. have just one or two drinks) and don't binge drink or let other people control what you drink

3 Understand alcohol units. A UK 'unit' is 10ml (2 tsp) of pure alcohol, and it's a measurement to do with how our body deals with alcohol. An average, healthy adult body (as opposed to yours) can break down 10ml (2 tsp) of alcohol in an hour. So, if an adult drinks 10ml (2 tsp) of alcohol, 60 minutes later there shouldn't be any left in their bloodstream. The problem is that the average drink has more than one unit. So if you drink a pint of cider you can have as

much as 3.4 units in your body that may affect you for up to 4 or 5 hours (depending on your size and weight).

4 Understand how alcohol works. It doesn't matter how much you eat, how much water you drink alongside alcohol, and whether you get hangovers or not, a unit of alcohol will always take an hour or more to leave your body. So, as long as it's in your body you are being affected by it.

5 If you feel you have a problem with alcohol, seek help from a parent or professional (see Resources).

Self-harming and your self-esteem

The umbrella term, self-harm, is used for a range of injuries people do to themselves to cope with distress. It can range from scratching to cutting oneself, picking and pulling skin and hair, and even branding oneself. People who self-injure are often seeking relief from emotional pain, and turn their misery on themselves. The episodes are usually in response to a trigger, such as a rejection, bullying or a friendship fallout.

Research shows that 10 per cent of 14- to 16-year-olds have self-harmed, and that girls are far more likely to self-harm than boys. The research also suggests that young people who self-harm are more likely to have low self-esteem, to be depressed and anxious. If this is happening to you:

1 You need to talk to someone about the problems you are facing. It's not 'weak' to feel unable to cope, so try to talk about your feelings with an adult you trust. Or a counsellor can help you (see Resources).

2 Work on building up your self-esteem. Self-harm is an expression of all your negative feelings towards yourself. It's not a sign that there is something wrong with you or that you are no good. Work on feeling good about who you are and challenging the parts of yourself that you consider negative.

3 Try to get to the root of why you feel so desperate. It can help to keep a note of when you self-harm and the feelings you have surrounding it.

4 Tell yourself you can stop and seek medical help for injuries.

Looking after your looks

Should something as frivolous as fashion and beauty be contained in a book about raising your self-esteem alongside all the serious stuff we've discussed so far? Well, yes it should, because taking care of the outside of yourself, making yourself look good so that you can feel good, is all part and parcel of having a healthy and buoyant self-esteem. There's nothing wrong with being into fashion, wanting to look nice and loving beauty products, as long as your expectations of what they can do for you are realistic (see Chapter Two for more on this).

Interestingly, girls with very low self-esteem tend to take less care of themselves in terms of beauty and fashion, primarily because:

- They don't see the point, as they don't believe they could look good.
- They don't feel they are worth the effort.
- They don't know where to start.
- They're afraid people will laugh if they try.
- They don't feel these markets cater to them.

The reality, however, is that the fashion and beauty markets cater to a wide range of people, despite the emphasis being on thin and perfect, which means it's there for the taking if you know how to make the best of it.

Finding your style

Whether you're into fashion or not, the way you dress tells the world how you feel about your body and who you feel you are. Dress in baggy clothes that hide your body and you're telling people you're embarrassed about how you look and that you're eager to hide away and feel at a low ebb about yourself. By comparison, wear something that shows off who you are, feels stylish, boosts your confidence and makes you want to stand tall. It will stop you feeling as if you've missed the fashion boat and need to hide away in a corner. Ask yourself this:

- Are your clothes hiding the real you?
- Do they represent you or something a magazine or a friend has told you to wear?
- Are you afraid to wear the stuff you like because you aren't thin or tall and/or your friends will laugh and make fun of you?
- Are you clueless about fashion?

Most people have experienced one if not all of the above at some point in their lives. So, here's what's important to know, if you want to look good in clothes and change your mindset about the outside of yourself:

1. You don't have to be thin to be fashionable and look good

'Thin equals fashionable' is a myth perpetrated by the media, and we feel it's true because 98 per cent of the people we see on TV and in magazines are thin. However, you can't blame the media completely if you feel this way, because the world around us *doesn't* show us this. If you feel that being thin is the only way to be fashionable, then you need to expand your idea of fashion and style.

Go for a walk and people-watch. Look for people who look amazing, different, confident and attractive, and note how they come in all shapes and sizes. Now, consider what you could do to be fashionable the way you are today. So this means, stop waiting until you feel thin enough or pretty enough to make the most of who you are. Do three things that change your look, whether it's wearing clothes that fit, wearing more colour or simply throwing away your favourite reliable 'fat' clothes (clothes we all have no matter what our size to hide behind when we don't feel good).

2. Knowing your body shape matters more than knowing your weight

Forget what size you are, or even what you weigh, because when it comes to looking good in clothes it's all down to dressing for your shape. This means knowing that what suits a curvy friend won't suit a pear-shaped one or a tall one. Knowing your own body shape is essential for this reason. Basically, body shapes tend to fall into three categories: pear shape, apple shape, and long and lean:

- Pear shapes are smaller on top, bigger on the bottom.
- Apple shapes are smaller on the bottom and legs. They are busty and have a bit of a tummy.
- Long and lean are, literally, long and lean.

However, be aware that you can be a mixture of shapes. So the following are just a stylist's basic clothes rules for you to experiment with:

Clothes that suit a pear shape are hipster jeans, A-line skirts that skim your lower half and fitted T-shirts. Wear patterns and colours on tops to emphasize the upper half.

Shapes that don't suit are short, tight skirts, which can make you look bigger below, and baggy tops; also hoodies that swamp you.

Clothes that suit apples are trousers and skirts that are straight, and so make you look longer. Try longer, looser T-shirts with V-necks, and shorter skirts.

Shapes that don't suit are baggy tops that make you look bustier, tops that are too tight and baggy jeans.

Clothes that suit long and lean are anything with a waist, straight legs and loose tops.

Shapes that don't suit are stretchy, tight tops, which will just cling to you; skirts that are too short with high heels will make you look too tall.

Having said all of the above, the only way you can work out how you're going to look and what you'll feel good in is to try on lots of different types of clothes. If you feel uncomfortable about doing this, enlist the help of a stylish friend for moral support. Often, people who have managed to get their own style right have an eye for getting it right for others.

3. You need to experiment with clothes

" My mum thinks I look ridiculous; my friends think I am out there, but I love the way I dress."
Sam, 13

Having just listed some ideas for anyone who is lost when it comes to what to wear, you can, of course, wear whatever you want, within reason, and probably should when you're experimenting with different looks. Part of having your own style is wearing things that you like, love and adore, as well as clothes that play to who you are; whether that's a type of music, a look similar to your favourite TV star, or something your friends all wear.

Whatever you choose to wear, you need to also be aware of what your clothes are telling the world about you. Some of this is about finding your style and working out what you love, against what looks good. Some of it is about wearing appropriate clothes at the right time. You don't need to be a brain surgeon to work that out, but you'd be surprised at how many people get it wrong.

Changing your look can have a large impact on the people around you. You may feel fantastically happy with your new-found style, but friends may feel jealous and try to get you to revert back to the old you. Also, your parents might be freaked out, especially if your new look is OTT and too sexy for your age. They may all try to get you to change what you're wearing and doing to yourself. What's important is to listen to what they are saying and work out if they are right or not before you make a decision for yourself.

> "I used to be a really baggy-jeans kind of girl, but over the summer I realised I like my legs and now wear a lot of skirts and high heels. Some of the girls in my class say I dress like a s*** just because I'm not dressing like them."
> **Tia, 14**

4. Good underwear is essential

Underwear is the support system for your clothes, and if you have good undies – that's a bra that fits your growing bust (see Chapter One for more on this) and good pants, you're on to a winner. If you don't, your clothes are going to look a little lacklustre, even if you get the right clothes for your shape and style.

It's not always easy asking your mum for money for underwear, especially if she's always been the one to buy it. Approach the subject with her, anyway, and see if you can at least choose a style you like (although choose within reason – G-strings and overly sexy bras will have your mother running from the shop).

5. Try creating a fashion board

Buy a load of magazines and go through them, cutting out any looks you like and any items of clothing, accessories and shoes you admire. Stick it all onto a board you can prop up in your room. Alongside your cuttings attach anything you like colour-wise and material-wise, and even add sayings and phrases. This is your idea board and it should help you to come up with lots of thoughts about what your look could possibly be and what your tastes are like.

The point of it isn't to replicate what you're seeing but to build up ideas for how you could perhaps create a similar look within your budget, with the clothes you already have and with perhaps help from family and friends.

A small aside: this is also a pretty good way to see if your fashion sense is out of kilter. If your board is full of super-skinny women wearing hugely expensive labels that you could never replicate, then it's a sign that you need to look at your beliefs around fashion, body image and beauty (see Chapter Two for more on this).

6. A style role model is essential

Most of us have a person in mind when we think of the words 'fashionable' and 'stylish', and even if this person is completely the opposite of you, they can teach you valuable lessons about style and help you to find your own. Ask yourself:

1 What is it about this person's style that sets them apart from others?
2 What do they do differently from other people that you admire?
3 What three things do you like about their look (not including their body shape)?
4 How have they changed their look?
5 What could you do to change your look?
6 What could you improve about your own look to improve how you feel about yourself (not including your body shape)?

If your role model is a celebrity, it's worth reminding yourself that very few celebrities dress themselves. Most employ a team of stylists who are experts who know how to dress other people. Their job is to create a look and dress celebrities from head to toe, including shoes, bags, jewellery and clothes. Which means that even your most favourite celebrity is probably pretty clueless and worried about getting it wrong when it comes to clothes.

7. Posture is core to looking good

Bad posture is an immediate low self-esteem giveaway. Think about it: when you feel embarrassed, under scrutiny, shy or under-confident how do you hold yourself? It's likely your shoulders slope, your arms wrap around you, your head drops low and you sink towards the floor. Or perhaps you're the queen of the angry look: chest puffed up, scowl on your face, fists semi-clenched and feet apart?

Whatever your posture (and it can help to look at old photos to see what your usual posture is), it pays to improve how you hold yourself, especially if you want to feel more confident and look good in clothes. Good posture does a number of things to you physically:

- It helps you to breathe more efficiently, because your shoulders are back and your head is up. Your voice instantly becomes stronger and you feel more confident.

- It makes you look taller and slimmer, as it puts you at your full height, and encourages you to hold yourself up using your stomach muscles.

- It makes you look more relaxed and feel more relaxed, because you're adopting a more normal stance.

The three exercises in the box overleaf are the key to good posture and you need to remind yourself of them when you're walking, standing and sitting. This is one area where watching models can really help, as they have fantastic posture and can teach you a lot about holding yourself in the right way.

Elongate and feel great!

1 The key to better posture is to start by imagining there is a string pulling you up from the top of your head. This should pull your head up and elongate your neck.

2 Next, imagine your shoulder blades sliding down your shoulders. This should roll your shoulders back and open your chest area. This can feel weird at first and possibly even make you feel vulnerable, but stay with it, as the feeling soon goes away.

3 Practise dropping your ribs and pulling your belly button gently towards your spine. Do this in a natural way or you'll never be able to maintain it. This is your body's support area and helps keep you upright. If you don't believe me, let it go and watch your body slump downwards.

8. Hair and make-up counts

Style isn't just about clothes and posture, it's also about how you look after the rest of you, such as your hair, skin and the way you wear make-up. Some girls with low self-esteem use their hair and make-up as a shield against the world. You will know what I mean if your hair is currently covering your face or your eyes or you use pots of make-up to cover up the real you.

Hair and make-up (if you wear any) should enhance your real beauty, not radically change it or hide you completely. The same goes for clothes and accessories such as jewellery. Signs you need to overhaul your hair and make-up are if people are constantly asking you to take your hair off your face or asking why you wear so much make-up. The key is to tone it down rather than going cold turkey. If you like make-up, but you are wearing it rather thickly, consider why you're wearing so much.

Is it to cover up bad skin? If so, it's worth knowing that make-up over bad skin hides relatively little. Work on applying less every day and seeing the response you get and how you feel about it. It can take time to get used to a more natural look, but in time it will boost your confidence about your real beauty rather than a manufactured one.

Many people use hair as something to hide behind, and it works, because if there is hair all over your face, no one can see the real you. If you're unsure how to experiment with a new look, try asking friends for help, or walk into a hairdresser's for a consultation. (This is where a hairdresser will tell you what they could possibly do with your hair and then you book an appointment for a later date.) Better still, flick through magazines and try to find a look that you can handle that isn't too radical but will still boost your confidence. The weird thing about hair is that often a simple haircut is all you need to do to overhaul your style completely (watch any TV makeover show to see this).

How to find your inner beauty

> "I don't do beauty. What's the point?
> I'm not beautiful on the inside or
> the outside."
> **Carly, 15**

The truth about beauty is that sometimes we all feel ugly. We wake up, our hair is standing up in ten directions, our face is blotchy and our eyes look weird. We seem to have gained 4.5kg (10lb) overnight and everything about us feels horrible and, as a result, we act in a horrible way. Maybe we do mean things, think hateful things or just go out of our way to spread the misery. It's something even the most beautiful women experience. Although it's normal, what's not normal is to feel like this all the time and never feel confident and assured that, despite the bad stuff, you're a beautiful person – someone to be valued both on the inside and out.

This is why having a sense of inner beauty is so important. If you know that inside you're someone who is a lovely person, you'll be able to like yourself even when you feel you've been struck overnight by the ugly stick! So, in a nutshell, inner beauty is thinking about what gives you a sense of satisfaction about yourself and your life and not being preoccupied with all the things that don't. Once you've located the facets of your inner beauty, it's about revelling in them, taking pleasure in them and enjoying them, because all these things are a fantastic reminder of all that is good about you, and your life, and something to hold on to when you're having a self-esteem wobble and feel like you're never going to like yourself again. To feel your inner beauty:

1 **Accept who you are**. This often means accepting the good stuff with the bad. So, step back and find things to feel beautiful about. Are you a kind person? Are your eyes sparkling? Does your hair give off a great shine? Are you funny, nice to others, smart and sharp? Whether you're all these things or more, try to enhance what is unique about you, and you'll come closer to feeling inner and outer beauty.

2 **Do beautiful things**. This means doing stuff for other people that makes them feel good, improves their self-esteem and boosts their confidence. Helping others to see the best in who they are is key to discovering the best in who you are. Plus, it will make you see that you have something good to offer the world.

3 **Make a beauty board**. Like the fashion board above, this should contain images and examples of things you find beautiful. It could be a picture of yourself as a baby, lyrics from a song, a picture of someone you know, a beautiful news story that touches your heart, a cartoon, a piece of material from a beautiful dress you once had, and so on. The idea is to look at this board every time you feel an ugliness-wave coming over you and remind yourself of all the things that make you feel a sense of inner beauty.

4 **Accept it's natural to feel threatened** by naturally beautiful girls. It tends to happen to us all, because coming across someone who turns heads makes us focus on our own shortcomings. This then fuels feelings

of inadequacy, competition and low self-esteem. What you have to remember is that someone's looks don't tell you anything about their lives or who they are. You're not in competition with them (unless you put yourself there) – and what impact does this really have on your life?

5 **Concede that you can only control so much**. In life you're sometimes not going to get what you want, and sometimes you're going to find that people don't like you (but that's OK because you're not going to like everyone you meet). These aren't things to stress about but to learn from. Just because someone doesn't want to be your friend it doesn't mean that you're not worthy or a good person. Just because you don't get what you want doesn't mean you're a failure.

6 **Remember that no one will ever look at you the way you look at yourself**. That's with such intensity and with so much negative judgement. This is good news, because it means you already know the person who judges you the hardest. The real test is if you can look at yourself in a kinder way and see yourself as others do.

7 **Appreciate what others think of you**. In all likelihood you are someone's daughter, someone's friend, someone's niece and maybe even someone's girlfriend. This means people love you and like you (even if it doesn't always feel that way) and that you are a worthwhile person who deserves to feel good about herself.

8 **Come to terms with your passions**, your peculiarities, quirks and odd habits that make you who you are, because it's these things that add to your inner beauty and show the world who you are. You may feel embarrassed by them or ashamed you feel the way you do, but how boring would the world be if we were all beautiful in the same way?

Being gorgeous for life

Hopefully, by now you'll know how to improve your self-esteem, bolster your body image and feel beautiful inside and out, but here are a few last words about feeling gorgeous for life. A healthy self-esteem fluctuates from high to low and back again, no matter how much work you put in. This means that some days you're going to be flying high and other days you may feel as if you're back at square one. When this happens it's important to remind yourself that you're fine and normal, but  also that you have the power to make yourself feel better and stronger. Remember that tomorrow will be a better day.

When you feel yourself flagging, stop and think about how you speak to yourself. Consider what's triggered you to feel the way you do, and then work on being more positive all round. This means stopping the negativity and self-criticism when you're having a bad day/week/month and basically giving yourself a much-needed break, or a hug or some respect.

Try practising the tips below on a regular basis, as they will help you to be vigilant about what you're saying, doing or thinking so that you don't slip back into what's known as 'autopilot thinking'.

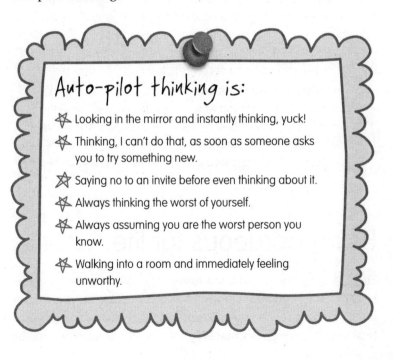

Auto-pilot thinking is:

- Looking in the mirror and instantly thinking, yuck!
- Thinking, I can't do that, as soon as someone asks you to try something new.
- Saying no to an invite before even thinking about it.
- Always thinking the worst of yourself.
- Always assuming you are the worst person you know.
- Walking into a room and immediately feeling unworthy.

Consider where your beliefs are coming from

Everything we believe about who we are comes from beliefs we have formulated from childhood onwards. These are beliefs about how we need to get approval, what we have to do to be liked and how 'good' we think we have to be in order to be loved. Most of these core beliefs are focused around issues that we find hard on an ongoing basis, such as feeling good enough, and tend to be reinforced by the things that happen to us, such as our interactions with family, friends and people in the outside world.

> "My sister always makes me feel bad. She just has to give me a look and I know she's thinking she's prettier and smarter than me. It's worse because I know she's right, it makes me feel really horrible about myself."
> **Sam, 13**

The problem with core beliefs is that they are incredibly strong but often not right. Sometimes they are illogical or off-centre, which is why you need to look at them and consider if they are driving you in a good way or a bad one. If, for example, you consistently believe you are stupid, stop and consider how true this belief is:

- Who first said you were stupid?
- What evidence do you have to back this belief up?
- What evidence disproves it totally?
- What do you get from believing you're stupid (we never believe something negative and painful unless it gives us a positive reward, such as attention or love, and so on)?

To put your beliefs in perspective you have to keep challenging what you believe. For example, are you really stupid just because you find homework difficult or because a parent or a teacher tells you this? What talents and skills do you have that show you're smart? What examples do you have of smart behaviour? What would you say to a friend who said this about herself, and how would you make her feel better?

Change your internal dialogue

This is the voice in your head that says all the mean things to you, such as: 'You're fat', 'You're horrible', 'You're not a nice person', 'No one likes you', 'You're a fake'. We all have this internal voice that brings us down, and it gets quieter the stronger our self-esteem becomes. So, to build belief, or to reboot it, you need to keep changing the record and replacing negative comments with positive ones.

> "I always used to tell myself I was a horrible person because I said mean things. Then my best friend reminded me that everyone does that and not everyone can be mean."
> **Charlotte, 14**

This doesn't, however, mean just playing lip service – you think you look awful but try to persuade yourself you look amazing. It means really finding a positive to replace the negative and saying it out loud. For example:

Negative voice: 'You look really ugly today.'

Positive voice: 'I look fine – my hair looks good, my eyes are nice and I quite like these jeans.'

Negative voice: 'You're such a fake.'

Positive voice: 'I'm a good person, because my friends like me and I'm always myself with them.'

It takes time to do this, so don't give up if it feels weird at first, after all it's taken you years to get comfortable with your negative voice. Practise every day and try to do it every time you hear your internal dialogue pop up with something demoralising, depressing and nasty.

Face your fears

> "I used to be terrified of answering a question in class. Partly from a fear of speaking up, but also out of fear that I'd be wrong and humiliate myself. When I made myself do it, I was on such a high, I don't know whether what I said was right or wrong, and I didn't care."
>
> **Scarlett 13**

You don't know what you can do until you try, but the problem is that most of us with low self-esteem give up before we try, and even when our self-esteem gets better it can be hard to override this tendency. In order to build confidence in your abilities you have to challenge yourself to face your fears. The good news is that this doesn't mean running naked across the school football pitch or asking someone out but facing the fears that make you feel anxious and afraid.

Write a list of your top five fears, with your biggest fear at the top and your smallest fear at the bottom.

Top five fears

1 _____

2 _____

3 _____

4 _____

5 _____

Now take your smallest fear and work on conquering it, whether it's making eye contact with teachers when you talk, breaking out of wearing black, or telling a friend you don't like the way she talks to you. Bear in mind that when you attempt to face this fear it's going to feel uncomfortable at first and you're going to feel shaky, but confidence and belief in yourself is built with small steps like this.

Each time you conquer a fear make sure you reinforce it by repeating it whenever you can until it becomes second nature to you and no longer something you're afraid of. The aim is to work your way up your fear list, taking your time to reinforce each kind of behaviour so that you can feel yourself getting stronger and stronger.

Have goals

"My goal is to be a writer, so I read loads of books, try to write stuff for the school paper and have been emailing writers I love, to see if they can help me."
Andie, 12

Accomplishment is the key ingredient to gaining continuous self-confidence, but you can't accomplish anything if you don't first have goals to aim for. Being goal orientated is about knowing what you want in life and how you're going to get there. If, for example, your goal is to have a social life and start having fun, sitting on the couch watching TV reruns will not move you closer to it. You have to motivate yourself and be passionate about your goals in order to make them happen.

To set goals:

1 First, base them on your priorities. What is the main goal/desire in your life right now? Is it to feel better about yourself, get on the netball team, make new friends or get healthy? The one you want the most is the one to start with.

2 Next, be specific about how you're going to get there. How, for example, are you going to make new friends or get healthy? Write a list, ask a friend or family member for help, and research it online.

3 What three things can you set in motion right now to make that goal happen? If it's new friends you're after, could you join an after-school class, get involved in an online forum, or volunteer? To get healthy, could you take up a new activity, ditch the junk food, talk to your mum about having healthier meals at home?

4 Finally, make sure you have a clear picture of what you want to achieve and are being realistic. Are you looking to make two new friends or 20? Are you hoping to be a size zero or be able to run for a bus without passing out?

Move out of your comfort zone

The comfort zone is the area we all make sure we stay in where we don't feel challenged or anxious or a little bit scared. It's a safe place to be, but it's also a place that ensures we don't grow in confidence.

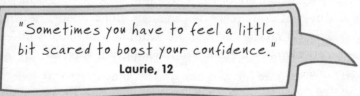

"Sometimes you have to feel a little bit scared to boost your confidence."
Laurie, 12

Think about actions that will take you just a little out of your comfort zone, such as public speaking or a writing group or joining the drama group – or even answering questions in class.

Remember, you're in the comfort zone if you:

- Feel safe where you are.
- Want to achieve more, but you're afraid to move from where you feel comfortable.
- Live in the 'I'll do it when I'm slimmer/older/happier/richer' frame of mind.

To help yourself, list three things you always tell yourself you're going to do when you are slimmer/older/happier/richer and then think about how you could do it now. For example:

Old promise:

1 **I'll get fit when I am slimmer.**
New way of thinking:
- I will get fit now by walking to school every day.
- I will get fit now by not skipping PE every week.

2 **I'll stand up to my friends when I feel more confident.**
New way of thinking:
- I will stand up to my friends by telling them when they are being mean.
- I will stand up to my friends by keeping away from them if they are not nice to me.

Be externally focused

To stop agonising about your flaws and what's wrong with you and why you don't feel good enough, think about throwing yourself into an outside venture. Nothing will make you feel better about yourself quicker than seeing how you can improve someone else's life.

If that doesn't grab you, try:

- Taking a class and learning something new that is useful or interesting. It could be a new language or how to decorate your room (try online courses or free online videos).

- Better still, do a daring feat for charity, such as a 5km (3 mile) run or a long sponsored walk. Organising your friends and getting people involved will do wonders for how you feel about yourself.

- Volunteer at a dog shelter or charity, or help someone you know by offering to do chores or shopping, or even babysitting for them.

- Find a role model you admire (for more than looks or fame) and read as much about them as you can. See what it teaches you about your own life.

> "I realise now how self-absorbed I used to be and how this made me really anxious and worried all the time. I now try to do things where I have to focus on other people, and it's helped me to be much happier."
>
> **Zoe, 14**

Less thinking, more doing

It may not feel like it, but life is a series of choices. So, what happens to you is not down to fate, destiny or chance. It's a process of accepting what you can't change and changing what you have power over. This means that sitting around complaining that life's not fair will get you precisely nowhere.

If you want to feel better and that you're accomplishing something, the key is: less thinking, more doing. If, for example, you love fashion but aren't wired to be a model, you can stop moaning that it isn't fair and instead take action and find a way to get into the industry. Think about designing, buying, textile design, being a personal shopper. The list of what you could do against what you couldn't do is endless. To help yourself:

1 Notice when you're having a thought that will cause you to be anxious, to worry and spiral into depression about your life.

2 Immediately tell yourself to stop thinking this and replace the thought with one that makes you feel good (a happy memory, a success, a nice compliment all work here).

3 Throw yourself into activity to change your mindset (dancing to loud music, having a bath, and even going for a walk will all help).

4 Do three positive things right now that make you feel good about your life and who you are.

> "I used to be a right moaner, always complaining that no one took me seriously about wanting to be an actress. Then one day my mum said it was because I'd never acted in anything, and maybe if I wanted people to take notice I should join a drama group or do the school play. She was right, of course."
> **Leah, 14**

Learn to be resilient

This is also known as learning to bounce back and to keep bouncing back. Talk to any successful person you know (or read about them), and no matter how successful they are it's likely they have had endless setbacks, but they've bounced back from them. Resilience is the key to ongoing self-belief and good self-esteem, because it's about moving forwards not stagnating where you are when things go wrong.

It's OK and normal to feel sorry for yourself, to cry and even stamp your feet when you're heartbroken or when a dream you've been after doesn't go to plan. However, picking yourself up and starting again is what will make you feel better and improve the situation.

Research shows that one factor that separates the resilient teens from the not-so-resilient ones is the ability to solve problems and set goals. So, instead of just being upset when something goes wrong, make sure you start problem solving:

1 Be aware of why you're upset, and think: How is this incident making me feel – and why?

2 Next, consider what you can learn from what went wrong.

3 Remind yourself that although you can't control the situation, you can control how you respond to what has happened to you.

4 Finally, put things into perspective. So, despite what has happened, remind yourself of all you have to be grateful for, and use that to motivate yourself to get up and try again.

Nurture your own self-esteem

Don't always seek a self-esteem boost outside of yourself, via boys, friends or parents. Asking for reassurance is fine, but needing constant support that you're nice/beautiful/clever is boring for others and is like sticking a plaster over a deep wound. The only way to bring your self-esteem to a healthy level is to find ways you can make yourself feel confident and smart and beautiful. That's by:

1 Identifying your strengths and talents, and allowing yourself to feel good about them.

2 Taking responsibility for your own happiness and not blaming your feelings or a bad day on your mum or the boy you fancy, or the fact that all models are thin.

3 Forgiving yourself for your mistakes and embarrassments – none of us are perfect, so give yourself a break.

4 Being good to yourself (see below for more on this). After all, if you can't treat yourself nicely, how will you ever let someone else treat you well?

Realise that everyone worries about not being liked

The secret no one ever tells you is that everyone (even people with excellent self-esteem) go through moments when they feel inferior and scared about being singled out and excluded, whether it's for what they say, what they look like or who they are. Why? Well, because we all want to be liked and accepted, even by the people we don't know – it's simply human nature.

The trick is to realise that thinking like this is 100 per cent normal, and then move on. Don't ponder the thought, don't make it come true (by acting as if you are inferior) and don't let it bring you down. The way to do this is by:

1 Faking it to make it. If you're in a social situation that's giving you the jitters, take a deep breath, jump in and get involved. It will take your mind off worrying what others think.

2 Keep things in perspective. Other people aren't constantly thinking about you or how you look, they are too busy worrying about themselves.

3 Stop worrying. Worrying is something we do when we feel helpless – it makes us feel as if we're in control when we're not and all it really does is increase anxiety levels.

4 Instantly think about a time when you felt confident and successful. Just recalling the feeling will help confidence to surge through you.

Finally, be your own best friend and like yourself. If you walk around feeling that you're so vile you deserve to be kicked, that's how the world will treat you. Fat, thin, pretty, unusual looking, tall, short or round – it pays to be proud of who you are, warts and all.

That's a tall order, I know, but you can do it, because countless other people have done the same before you. Remember: you don't have to choose to view yourself as a failure that no one likes or admires. Instead you can give yourself a break, take a deep breath and love who you are: the good bits, the bad bits, the ugly bits and, of course, the gorgeous bits that are just dying to come out!

Resources

Anger management

British Association of Anger Management
www.angermanage.co.uk
Offering support, programmes and training for
parents, children and teenagers.

Bullying

Bullying UK
www.bullying.co.uk

Kidscape
www.kidscape.org.uk Tel: 08451 205 204
Helping to prevent bullying – advice and information.

Confidential helplines

Childline
www.childline.org.uk Tel: 0800 1111

Get Connected
www.getconnected.org
Tel: 0808 8084 994 (1.00pm–11.00pm)
A confidential national helpline for
young people under 25, which helps
them to work out what they need most.
It can put them in touch with places that
can help – whatever the issue.

Domestic violence

Women's Aid National Domestic Violence Helpline
www.womensaid.org.uk
Tel: 0808 2000 247 (freephone 24-hour national helpline)
Women's Aid is the national charity working to end domestic
violence against women and children.

Drinking and drugs

FRANK
www.talktofrank.com Helpline, tel: 0800 776600
Ring FRANK anytime and speak to a friendly adviser who's
professionally trained to give you straight up, unbiased
information about drugs and alcohol.

Eating, weight and self-esteem

Dove
www.dove.co.uk
The Dove Self-Esteem Fund and website
was developed to help girls break free
from self-limiting beauty stereotypes.

BEAT (Beat Eating Disorders)
www.b-eat.co.uk Tel: 0845 634765
(Formerly Eating Disorders
Association) BEAT provides advice and
support for anyone with an eating disorder,
including anorexia and bulimia nervosa.

MEND
www.mendprogramme.org
MEND (Mind, Exercise, Nutrition ... Do it!) is an organisation
dedicated to reducing global childhood overweight and obesity
levels. The MEND Programme was devised at Great Ormond
Street Hospital for Children and the University College London
Institute of Child Health. There are more than 300 programmes
across the UK.

Shine 4 U

www.shine4u.org

SHINE (Self Help Independence, Nutrition and Exercise) aims to help obese young people, not only to lose weight but also to develop a range of skills to increase in confidence and self-esteem. This enables young people to make more permanent changes to their lifestyles and to become a healthier and fitter person, both physically and mentally.

Eating well

www.eatwell.gov.uk

Food Standards Agency healthy-eating website.

Health issues

Quit

www.quit.org.uk

A charity that aims to help smokers quit smoking.

The Site

www.thesite.org

Provides information and advice on a range of issues affecting young adults aged 16–25.

Teenage Health Freak

www.teenagehealthfreak.org

Information and advice on a variety of teen issues.

Parents

Growing Kids

www.growingkids.co.uk

Growing Kids was formed to offer a unique reference point on information and advice for parents of growing kids.

Parentline Plus

www.parentlineplus.org.uk Tel: 0808 800 2222

A national charity, that works for, and with, parents offering help, advice and information on parenting issues.

Self harm

Bristol Crisis Service for Women
Tel: 0117 925 1119
Support service for women and girls in emotional distress,
especially those who self-harm.

National Self-Harm Network
www.nshn.co.uk

SANEline
www.sane.org.uk Tel: 0845 767 8000
Offers emotional support and information to anyone
experiencing stress, mental health problems or self-harm.

Australia

Eating Disorders Foundation Inc (EDF) EDF Inc.
www.edf.org.au
Aims to provide sufferers of eating disorders and their families
and friends with up-to-date information about the various
eating disorders and about services and resources to assist
recovery.

Kids Helpline
www.kidshelp.com.au Tel: 1 800 55 1800
Kids Help Line is Australia's only free, confidential and
anonymous, telephone and online counselling service
specifically for young people aged between five and 25.

New Zealand

Central Region Eating Disorders Services
www.eatingdisorders.org.nz

Headspace
www.headspace.org.nz/young-people/eating-problems.htm
For young people in Auckland and all over New Zealand, as well

as their families and schools. Offering help and advice on a large range of subjects, such as stress, family problems and school.

Canada

Kids Help Phone
www.kidshelpphone.ca Tel: 1 800 668 6868
Kids Help Phone is Canada's only toll-free, national, bilingual, phone and Web counselling, referral and information service for children and youth. They provide immediate anonymous and confidential support, 24 hours a day, 365 days a year.

National Eating Disorder Information Centre
www.nedic.ca
Tel: toll-free 1-866-NEDIC-20 (1-866-633-4220)

America

American Dietetic Association
www.eatright.org Tel: (800) 877-1600
The American Dietetic Association offers nutrition news, tips, resources for consumers and dieticians, and a find-a-nutritionist search tool.

MyPyramid.gov
www.mypyramid.gov
The US government's website about the MyPyramid Plan Food Guidance System features information on the food pyramid and its 12 models geared to different people, online tools, and dietary guidelines.

Kids Health
www.kidshealth.org
Informative teen website on health, weight and emotions.

Self-esteem

Dove
www.dove.com
American site for the Dove Self-Esteem Fund.

Teen Line
www.teenlineonline.org/teens (310) 855-HOPE (4673)
Teen Line is a confidential telephone helpline for teenaged
callers. It operates every evening from 6.00pm until 10.00pm
and is toll-free from anywhere in California. If you have a
problem or just want to talk with another teen that
understands, then this is the right place for you. Teen Line
also offers email help, online chat, message boards, resources
and information.

Index

acne 29–31, 75
action-focused approach 152–3
advertising 7, 8, 70, 73, 75
airbrushing 73
alcohol intake 131–3
alcohol units 132–3
anger 39–40, 104–5
  management 39–40
anorexia nervosa 62–4
antiperspirants 28
anxiety 117, 119, 120–1
appetite 17
apple shapes 136
approval seeking 45–6, 119, 154
auto-pilot thinking 145

bacteria, and body odour 27, 29
bad breath 131
bad habits 130–4
ballet 62
beauty 70–80
  boards 144
  care 134, 141–2
  ideals 71, 74
  industry 73, 74–7
  inner 142–4
  quiz 71–2
  and smoking 131
'being dumped' 114–15
bikini waxes 24
binge drinking 132
'bingeing and purging' 64
black-and-white thinking 68
body 5–40
  blaming your 68–9
  body hair 22–5
  body odour 27–9

breast development 18–22
  dissatisfaction with your 6–7,
    13–14, 17, 41–3, 46–51, 67, 77
  looking after your 122–34
  loving your 5–6
  periods 25–7
  spots 29–31
body fat 16–18
  see also fat, feeling you are
body hair 23–5, 28
body image 41–80, 122–3
  assessing your 43–6
  and beauty 70–80
  and body shape 46–51
  changing fashions in 48–9
  definition 43
  development exercise 69–70
  and diets 51–4
  and eating disorders 62–4
  and feeling you are fat 56–62
  improving 64–70, 78–80
  making the most of yourself 66–8
  media ideals 47, 49–50
  negative influences on 42–3, 46–64,
    70–7
  and peer groups 54–5
body odour 27–9
body shape 46–51, 65–6, 136–7
  apple shapes 136
  dressing for your 61
  ectomorphs 65
  endomorphs 65–6
  'long and lean' types 136–7
  mesomorphs 65
  obsessing about 46–51
  pear shapes 136
  quiz 47–8

boys 110–16
  'being dumped' 114–15
  and puberty 10–11
  quizzes on 111–12
  and sex 115
bras 20, 138–39
breasts
  development 14, 15, 18–22
  exercises for 19
  lopsided 21
  nipples 22
  normal 18–19, 21
bulimia nervosa 62–3, 64
bullying 89–96

caffeinated drinks 125
celebrities
  style 140
  super-thin 62
cellulite cream 76
cliques 82–9
clothing
  experimenting with 137–8
  fashion boards 139
  and parents 108–9
  and posture 140–1
  and puberty 10, 11, 17
  and role models 139–40
  style 135–41
  underwear 138–9
  and your body shape 61
comfort zones 150–1
comparison making 21, 78, 143–4
compliments, accepting 69–70
confidence 78
controlling behaviour
  handling your own 144
  of parents 108–9
core beliefs 146–7
cosmetic surgery 77, 79
counselling 37, 91

decision-making 152–3
depression 28

diet, balanced/healthy 53, 123–7
  and portion size 126
  and puberty 17
  rules for 125, 126–7
diet pills 53
diets/dieting
  and body image 51–4
  crash diets 54
  dietary restrictions 54
  low-calorie diets 54
  low-fat diets 54
DNA (deoxyribonucleic acid) 11
Dove 7

eating disorders 62–4
ectomorphs 65
emotion diaries 32–3
emotional triggers 33–5
emotions
  expression 39, 99, 104–5
  painful 133
  and puberty 31–40
  see also anger
empathy 98
endomorphs 65–6
endorphins 128
enemies 82–6, 89–95

facial hair 25
families 81–2, 100–9
  and body image 50–1
  overprotective parents 105–6, 107–8
  quiz 100–1
  top tips for handling 109
  and your core beliefs 146–7
fashion *see* clothing
fashion boards 139
fast foods 124–5
fat, dietary 124
fat, feeling you are 56–62
  see also body fat
fathers 106–9
fears, facing your 148–9
feet 29

focus
  action-based 152–3
  external 151–2
follicle stimulating hormone
    (FSH) 33
friends 81–100
  and dieting 53, 54–5
  friendship quiz 85–6
  improving friendship skills 98–100
  mean behaviour by 89–91
  popular girls 96–8
  who are enemies 91–5

generalisations 68
genes 11–12
goal setting 149–50, 154
gossip 100
growth hormones 15
growth spurts 13–17

habits, bad 130–4
hair 76–7, 141–2
hair bleach 25
hair removal 24–5, 28
  creams 24, 25
help seeking 37
helplessness 120
hormones
  growth 15
  and mood swings 14, 31–3
  and spots 29–30
hunger, rating your 126

inner beauty 142–4
internal dialogue 35, 147–8

judged, feeling 34–5, 36–7
junk food 124–5

kindness 143

labels 99–100
laser skin resurfacing 75
laxatives 53, 64

loneliness 95–6
'long and lean' types 136–7
love see boys

magazines 49–50
make-up 141–2
makeovers 79–80
meal-skipping 52, 126
mean behaviour 35–7, 89–91, 98, 142
media ideals, of the perfect body 47,
    49–50
menstruation (periods) 18, 25–7, 32
mesomorphs 65
mindsets, altering weight-obsessed 58
mistakes, making 121, 154
models 7, 8, 51, 62, 71, 73
Montgomery glands 22
mood swings 31–3
  and hormones 14, 31–3
  and periods 26–7
mothers 51, 82, 103–6

negative thought patterns 68–9
nicotine 131
nipples 22
  inverted 22

obesity 57, 61–2
oestrogen 33
'outsiders' 86, 93–6
over-achievers 118–19
over-sensitivity 119–20
overeating 59
overprotective parents 105–6, 107–8
overweight 57, 59–62

PE (Physical Education) 127
pear shapes 136
peer groups
  and body image 54–5
  and smoking 130
people pleasers 86, 99, 119
perfectionism 98, 117–18
periods (menstruation) 25–7, 32

and mood changes 26–7
onset 18
and smoking 131
personal hygiene 28
personal responsibility, taking 154
personal strengths 60
physical exercise 60, 127–30
compulsive 130
plastic surgery 77, 79
popularity, worrying about 96–8, 155
portion sizes 126
posture 140–1
pre-menstrual syndrome (PMS) 26–7,
131
priorities 150
problem solving 154
puberty
and body hair 22–5
and body odour 27–9
and boys 10–11
and breast development 18–22
defining 8–12
early 9, 10
emotional changes of 31–40
and feeling tired 15
feeling unhappy about 13–16, 17
late 9, 10
onset 9, 12
and periods 25–7
physical changes of 16–18
public nature of 14–15
and self-doubt 15–16
and self-esteem 12–16, 32
and spots 29–31
pubic hair 23, 24

quizzes
beauty image 71–2
body shape 47–8
boys 111–12
family issues 100–1
friend issues 85–6
self management 116–17
self-esteem in puberty 12–13

weight-obsession 57–8
reflections, feelings about 67–8
resilience 153–4
role models 7, 64–5, 105, 139–40
romance see boys
Roosevelt, Eleanor 81

saturated fat 124
scars, acne 75
self
dealing with your 116–21
making the most of your 66–8
self-acceptance 66–8, 121, 143, 144
self-appreciation 66–8
self-belief 146–7
self-care 60–1, 155
self-destructive behaviour 37, 41,
133–4
self-esteem 1–3, 35, 41–2, 122–3
and alcohol 131–3
assessing your 43–6
and beauty care 134, 141
and body dissatisfaction 42
and boys 109–14
and cliques 88
definition 42
developing 46, 69, 154
and dieting 52–3
and family and friends 82–4, 98–9,
102–4, 108–9
natural fluctuations in 144–55
negative influences on 42–3
and over-achieving 119
and over-sensitivity 119–20
and perfectionism 117
and periods 26
and physical exercise 127–30
and posture 140
and puberty 12–16, 32
and self-destructive behaviour 37,
41, 133–4
signs of low 45
and smoking 130
self-forgiveness 121, 154

self-fulfilling prophecies 104–5
self-harm 37, 41, 133–4
self-hate 39–40
separation-individuation 35–7
sex 115
sexism 109, 115
shame 91
shaving 24, 25, 28
shoes 29
sidekicks 88–9
'size zero' 61–2
skin
  care 75, 130
  spots 29–31, 75
sleep requirements 15
smoking 130–1
social competence 83
social situations 81–121
  boys 109–16
  cliques 82–9
  enemies 82–6, 89–95
  families 50–1, 81–2, 100–10, 146–7
  friends 53, 54–5, 81–100
  managing yourself in 116–21
  peer groups 54–5, 131
social support 60
sport 70, 127–9
spots 29–31, 75
stretch marks 19
stretch-mark creams 76
style 135–42
success 60
sugar 124–5
sweat 27–9
sweat glands
  apocrine 27, 29
  eccrine 27

talents 60
teeth
  perfect white 77
  smoking and your 131
thinness
  and being fashionable 135–6
  ideals of 8, 47
thought patterns
  auto-pilot thinking 145
  black-and-white thinking 68
  negative thinking 68–9
threatened feelings 143–4
tiredness 15
TV programmes, and body image 50

ugly, feeling 79–80
underwear 20, 138–9

vaginal deodorants 28
vaginal douches 28
vaginal infections 28
vomiting 53, 64

water retention 27
waxing 24–5
weight
  feeling you are fat 56–62
  gain 16–18, 27, 124
  normal 54, 55
  overweight 57, 59–62
  and smoking 130
  see also body fat; thinness
weight-obsession 56, 57–8
'whole person', seeing yourself as 62,
    67–8, 121
worrying 120, 155
wrinkles, premature 131